TIMSS 2015 GRADE 9
National Report

Understanding mathematics and science
achievement amongst Grade 9 learners
in South Africa

Linda Zuze, Vijay Reddy, Mariette Visser, Lolita Winnaar, Ashika Govender

HSRC
PRESS

Published by HSRC Press
Private Bag X9182, Cape Town, 8000, South Africa
www.hsrcpress.ac.za

First published 2017

ISBN (soft cover) 978-0-7969-2502-2
ISBN (pdf) 978-0-7969-2491-9

The publishers have no responsibility for the continued existence or accuracy of URLs for external or third-party Internet websites referred to in this book and do not guarantee that any content on such websites is, or will remain, accurate or appropriate.

Copy-edited by Purple Frog Communications
Typeset by Purple Frog Communications
Cover design by Purple Frog Communications
Printed by CAPiTiLPRESS, Cape Town, South Africa

Distributed in Africa by Blue Weaver
Tel: +27 (0)21 701 4477; Fax Local: (0)21 701 7302; Fax International: 0927865242139
www.blueweaver.co.za

Distributed in Europe and the United Kingdom by Eurospan Distribution Services (EDS)
Tel: +44 (0)17 6760 4972; Fax: +44 (0)17 6760 1640
www.eurospanbookstore.com

Distributed in North America by River North Editions, from IPG
Call toll-free: (800) 888 4741; Fax: +1 (312) 337 5985
www.ipgbook.com

Acknowledgements

The Trends in International Mathematics and Science Study (TIMSS) is a four-year project. There were numerous components to the TIMSS project that many people contributed towards in order to complete this project. We acknowledge the efforts of these individuals and institutions.

- The Department of Basic Education (DBE) for the funding and support for the successful implementation of this research study;

- The provincial coordinators who facilitated access to schools;

- The school principals, educators and learners who participated in the study;

- The Human Sciences Research Council (HSRC) research team: Vijay Reddy, Fabian Arends, Cas Prinsloo, Mariette Visser, Lolita Winnaar, Andrea Juan and Shawn Rogers;

- The Education and Skills Development administrative team: Matselane Maja, Elmi de Koning, Erika Masser and Maria Ngema for their work in organising the massive surveys and providing support to all aspects of the project;

- Pontsho Wiseman Thaba for assistance with the Cross-Country Scoring Reliability and the Trend Scoring Reliability activities;

- Pearson South Africa, the data collection agency;

- Quality assurance of the data collection process: Azinga Tele, Catherine Namome, Genevieve Haupt, Kholofelo Motha, Lisa Wiebesiek, Maglin Moodley, Matthews Makgamatha, Mogege Mosimege, Nosisi Feza, Sylvia Hannan, Tamlynne Meyer and Shawn Rogers;

- Jaqueline Harvey and Unathi Beku for research assistance on the project;

- Short-term contract staff who assisted with administrative tasks and assessment scoring;

- Vanessa Scherman, Caroline Long, Corene Coetzee and Amelia Abrie for contributing by using TIMSS performance data to create relevant benchmarks for South Africa; and

- Surette van Staden and Martin Gustaffson for critical review of the report.

Dr Vijay Reddy
TIMSS National Research Coordinator
Human Sciences Research Council

Contents

List of figures

List of tables

List of acronyms

CAPS	Curriculum Assessment Policy Statements
DBE	Department of Basic Education
DG	Director-General
DME	Data Management Expert
DoE	Department of Education
DPC	Data Processing Centre
DPME	Department of Planning, Monitoring and Evaluation
ECD	Early Childhood Development
HLM	Hierarchical Linear Modelling
HSRC	Human Sciences Research Council
ICC	Intraclass correlation coefficient
ICT	Information and communication technology
IEA	International Association for the Evaluation of Educational Achievement
IIAL	Incremental Introduction of African Languages
IRT	Item response theory
LoLT	Language of learning and teaching
LTSM	Learning and Teaching Support Material
MTSF	Medium Term Strategic Framework
NATED	National Accredited Technical Education Diploma
NCV	National Certificate Vocational
NDP	National Development Plan
NQF	National Qualifications Framework
NSC	National Senior Certificate
NSMSTE	National Strategy for Mathematics, Science and Technology Education
NSNP	National School Nutrition Programme
OECD	Organisation for Economic Co-operation and Development
PISA	Programme for International Student Assessment
SACMEQ	Southern and Eastern Africa Consortium for Monitoring Educational Quality
SDGs	Sustainable Development Goals
SE	Standard Error
SES	Socioeconomic status
SET	Science, Engineering and Technology
SGB	School Governing Body
STEM	Science, Technology, Engineering and Mathematics
TIMSS	Trends in International Mathematics and Science Study
WinW3S	Windows Within-School Sampling Software

Executive summary

South Africa has participated in five cycles of the Trends in International Mathematics and Science Study (TIMSS), beginning in 1995. The 2015 TIMSS Grade 9 study was administered in August 2015 by a team of researchers at the Human Sciences Research Council (HSRC) in collaboration with the Department of Basic Education (DBE) and the International Association for the Evaluation of Educational Achievement (IEA). Results of the 2015 TIMSS Grade 9 study are presented in this report. The focus areas for TIMSS are mathematics and science. This report also takes stock of past results in an effort to improve our understanding of what is required to improve academic performance in mathematics and science.

TIMSS follows a two-stage stratified cluster sampling design. The TIMSS 2015 sample was explicitly stratified by province, type of school (public and independent schools) and language of learning and teaching (LoLT) (English, Afrikaans and dual medium). The realised sample included 292 principals, 331 science teachers, 334 mathematics teachers and 12 514 learners. In addition to the learner assessment data, the study also collected contextual information from learners, teachers and school principals, making it possible to explore the factors that are related to Grade 9 mathematics and science achievement.

Three analytical approaches are used in this report in order to maximise the value of the TIMSS study for policy and practice. The first approach is descriptive in nature and provides an overview of achievement in mathematics and science based on where learners live and learn. The second approach is inferential and employs multilevel modelling techniques to explore contextual factors associated with learner achievement. The final approach uses item response theory (IRT) to compare what learners know to what they are expected to know based on the local curriculum. National proficiency benchmarks have been developed that are more closely aligned to the South African educational system. This is the first time that the TIMSS national report has constructed and reported on national proficiency benchmarks based on the TIMSS data. The findings that follow will be summarised based on the three analytical approaches.

Results of descriptive analysis of trends (2003 to 2015)

Between TIMSS 2003 and 2011, the mathematics and science scores improved by 67 and 64 points respectively. Between 2011 and 2015, the mathematics and science scores improved by a further 20 and 26 points respectively. The highest gains were achieved at the lower end of the achievement distribution, which is indicative of reduced inequality. The results also show that when compared to other countries who participated in both the 2003 and 2015 cycles, South Africa has shown the largest change in performance, although it is acknowledged that South Africa started from a very low base.

The number of schools and learners in the TIMSS sample permits reliable estimates of provincial performance. Looking at the provincial results, Gauteng and the Western Cape were the top performing provinces in 2015 and had mean scores above the national average of 372 and 358 in mathematics and science respectively. The Eastern Cape together with North West and Limpopo were the three lowest-achieving provinces. However, Limpopo showed the largest positive change, followed by Gauteng and the Eastern Cape. In 2003 the score difference between the highest- and lowest-performing provinces was 205 points. This provincial gap has narrowed considerably to 77 points in 2015, which is another indication of improved equity in the education system.

As part of the government's pro-poor strategy to support education, schools in quintiles 1, 2 and 3 receive subsidies that make it possible to exempt learners from paying fees. Thus, public schools are categorised into no-fee (quintiles 1, 2 and 3) and fee-paying schools (quintiles 4 and 5). Of the learners who participated in TIMSS 2015, 65 per cent attended no-fee schools, 31 per cent fee-paying schools and four per cent were from independent schools. The average mathematics and science scores for each of the school types are significantly different, with no-fee schools recording the lowest performance. The results, however, show how the increases in TIMSS scores from 2011 to 2015 play out differently across the different school types, with learners in public schools achieving the largest gains. The achievement scores of learners who attended no-fee schools increased by 17 and 23 points for mathematics and science, respectively. Learners who attended fee-paying schools increased their average scores by 26 and 31 points for mathematics and science, respectively. Learners who attended independent schools increased their scores by 4 and 6 points for mathematics and science, respectively. Average scores in each school type were still below the TIMSS centre point of 500 in 2015.

There have been steady improvements in learner access to basic amenities but the gap in home resources between learners in the no-fee and fee-paying components of the education system remains wide.

A learner's background and home environment can influence academic outcomes. Nationally, 51 per cent of learners are the appropriate age for the grade, but the picture looks very different when the results are disaggregated by school type. In 2015, 43 per cent of Grade 9 learners in no-fee schools were age-appropriate compared to the 64 per cent and 73 per cent in fee-paying and independent schools, respectively. Language of learning and teaching (LoLT) is an important and complex aspect of mathematics and science education and the TIMSS results lend further support to the need to understand the role that language plays. Learners whose home language and LoLT are the same achieved higher mathematics and science scores than learners whose home language and LoLT differ. These gaps were wider for science because the curriculum relies more on reading and writing in science than in mathematics, where problem solving can be expressed in non-written formats.

There have been steady improvements in learner access to basic amenities but the gap in home resources between learners in the no-fee and fee-paying components of the education system remains wide. Ninety-four per cent of learners in independent schools had access to water-flush toilets at home in 2015 compared to 90 per cent of learners in fee-paying schools and only 44 per cent of learners in no-fee schools. Responses to questions about attitudes towards mathematics and science showed that learners attached a higher value to mathematics than to science, but confidence levels were low in both subjects. Only 10 per cent of Grade 9 learners expressed high levels of confidence in mathematics and science, and there was a decline in confidence levels between 2011 and 2015.

The report also looked at the support for learning that is available outside of school and included analysis of how often learners received homework, how often parents checked homework and whether parents were able to assist learners with homework. Learners who attended public schools received mathematics and science homework more often than learners attending independent schools. Learners received mathematics homework more often than science homework. Sixty-eight per cent of learners received mathematics homework every day compared to 23 per cent who received science homework. A higher percentage of learners in no-fee schools felt that their parents had difficulty assisting them with homework as a result of either the complexity of the homework or the language used to present the homework.

The report also focused on the schooling environment in terms of how school resources and school climate are related to performance. Access to adequate resources is of course necessary for teaching and learning, but the results showed that the school climate played a crucial role. In no-fee schools, a higher percentage of learners were exposed to a lower emphasis on academic success, teachers who were less satisfied with their jobs and principals who reported more widespread discipline and safety problems. It is also within these schools that being bullied was more common. Bullying was also prevalent in fee-paying and independent schools but the rates were considerably lower. Grade 9 learners in the South African study were also asked how often they were instigators of bullying. National results showed that at least 25 per cent of learners were perpetrators of different forms of bullying on a weekly basis. Filling teacher vacancies for both subjects was more difficult in no-fee schools than in fee-paying and independent schools. Thirty-one per cent of learners attended no-fee schools where it was difficult to fill mathematics vacancies compared to 16 per cent of learners in fee-paying schools and only three per cent of learners in independent schools. Schools faced similar challenges in filling science vacancies although it was more difficult to fill science vacancies than mathematics vacancies in independent schools.

Executive summary

Results of school effectiveness analysis

The second analytical approach that was used in this report was inferential in nature. It was concerned with why and how school characteristics are associated with mathematics achievement. Because of the nested or hierarchical nature of TIMSS data (Grade 9 learners within schools) and the nature of the research questions, a multilevel analytical approach was used. The benefit of this type of analysis is that it is possible to take into account learner background factors and isolate which school characteristics are associated with achievement. This type of inquiry also falls within a broader category of educational research called school effectiveness studies.

The ideal situation is for school quality to be high and for the differences between schools to be minimal. The 2015 results of the multilevel analysis showed that 61 per cent of the total variation in Grade 9 mathematics performance occurred between schools, which was an improvement from 64 per cent reported in TIMSS 2011. Although achievement differences between schools in developing countries can be large, the results for South Africa point to a particularly high level of inequality across schools in the education system. Schools with more resources to draw upon and better facilities devoted to education were at an advantage but the climate of learning played a unique and significant role in TIMSS Grade 9 achievement that went beyond access to resources. Because the analyses made use of cross-sectional data the ability to draw strong causal inferences was limited.

> Schools with more resources to draw upon and better facilities devoted to education were at an advantage but the climate of learning played a unique and significant role in TIMSS Grade 9 achievement that went beyond access to resources. Because the analyses made use of cross-sectional data the ability to draw strong causal inferences was limited.

Results of item analysis

This section described science achievement for Grade 9 learners using mean scores for the different content areas tested in TIMSS. National benchmarks and performance level descriptors were derived from a Rasch analysis of the South African science results. This process provided information about what South African learners know and can do at different points on the achievement scale. The descriptions of what learners can do in the different proficiency bands can help curriculum planners in designing appropriate interventions. Although the science results were used to demonstrate this method in this report, a full report containing both mathematics and science analyses is available separately. The TIMSS achievement instrument is designed to respond to the curricula of 39 countries. Further analysis showed that there is a high level of overlap with the South African Curriculum Assessment Policy Statements (CAPS), with 91 per cent of topic overlap and 81 per cent of item overlap. Compared to the overall average, performance was higher in the chemistry section and lower in the earth science section. Unlike their international counterparts, South African learners scored far lower than the overall average in knowledge items.

Key findings

1. *The value in participating in international assessments is increased when the results are used for understanding national conditions.* South Africa's participation in TIMSS over the last twenty years has enriched our understanding of learner performance and how the country is ranked relative to other

education systems around the world. Raising performance standards can improve a country's economic competitiveness; the global perspective is therefore an important one. South Africa's membership in the TIMSS community has also helped to develop the capacity of local researchers and increased the technical rigour of our large-scale assessments. The global perspective was supplemented by a national one. The South African analysis included the identification of a group of potential learners. These are learners who are close to the minimum competency benchmarks as defined by TIMSS. Additional Rasch analysis of the South African results can better inform policy makers about what mathematics and science skills Grade 9 learners have acquired.

2. *South African mathematics and science achievement scores have improved from a 'very low' (1995, 1999, 2003) to a 'low' (2011, 2015) national average.* South Africa is still one of the lower-performing countries in mathematics and science in comparison to other TIMSS participating countries. However, from 2003 to 2015 the country has shown the biggest positive improvement of all participating countries in both mathematics (by 90 points) and science (by 87 points), which is equivalent to an improvement in achievement by two grade levels. Average performance in the public school system and among historically weaker provinces has clearly improved, but most Grade 9 learners are yet to achieve a minimum level of competency in mathematics and science, based on the TIMSS international perspective.

3. *South African achievement continues to remain highly unequal but there has been a slight decline in inequality between schools over time.* Like other low-performing countries, only one-third of South African learners achieved a mathematics and science score above the benchmark of 400 points, a score denoting the minimum level of competence. When the achievement scores are broken down by school type, the patterns reveal vast inequalities. Approximately 80 per cent of learners attending independent schools, 60 per cent of learners at fee-paying and 20 per cent of learners at no-fee schools achieved mathematics scores above the minimum level of competency. Within this unequal performance, it is also worth noting that 3.2 per cent of South African mathematics learners and 4.9 per cent of science learners achieved mathematics and science scores at the high level of achievement (above 550 points).

4. *Almost half the Grade 9 learners in the school system are over-age.* The pattern is different based on school types, with 43 per cent of learners in no-fee schools, 64 per cent in fee-paying and 73 per cent in independent schools at the appropriate age. The achievement scores of over-age learners are much lower than those of age-grade appropriate learners, suggesting that simply spending an extra year in a grade is not leading to more learning. For grade repetition to lead to improved learning outcomes, repeat learners must receive extra learning support. This must start at the foundation phase, otherwise the performance levels will widen as learners progress through the education system.

5. *The importance of LoLT for mathematics and science goes further than previously considered in TIMSS.* The influence of language was evident throughout this study. The national benchmarking exercise emphasised that language skills were important for answering any item on the test regardless of the level of difficulty. At home, parents who were not fluent in the language of instruction struggled to provide homework support for their children. At school, less fluency in the language of the test (either English or Afrikaans) was related to lower test scores. Learners who spoke the language of the test more frequently, achieved better results and this was over and above the effect of socioeconomic status (SES). This implies that all learners, regardless of their SES, are disadvantaged by lack of language fluency. Moreover, fluency in the LoLT does not guarantee academic success. The language of mathematics and science in the classroom may present a completely different set of challenges if words that learners are familiar with take on a different meaning in the classroom context. Addressing the role of language is not easy nor is it quick. The goal is not to make learners more capable in the use of language simply for testing purposes but to ensure that they are better equipped to understand the nuances of the materials covered in mathematics and science.

Executive summary

6. *Resources matter but educational success goes beyond improving resource access.* There has been some improvement in terms of equalising home access to running tap water, water-flush toilets and electricity but learners from no-fee schools had the most limited access to home resources, with access to technology remaining exclusive to wealthier learners. The evidence on school resources was both heartening and disappointing. It was encouraging that physical resources had an independent and positive association with average school achievement as this means that policies that have worked to improve access to school resources can continue to play a positive role in improving educational quality. However, narrowing the achievement gap between no-fee, fee-paying and independent schools is not as simple as just improving resource access. Forty per cent of learners in fee-paying schools and 20 per cent of learners in independent schools failed to meet the minimum level of competency set by TIMSS. Maintaining the momentum around resource accessibility and efficient utility must continue but that this is only part of the solution for improving performance and equity between schools. Human resource challenges were greater in public schools and it was more difficult to fill vacancies in these environments. Strategies to recruit and retain the best subject-specific teaching professionals into public schools needs to continue.

7. *The climate of the school counts.* Schools with a healthier school climate (emphasis on academic success, safety and order, fewer disciplinary problems, fewer incidences of bullying and fewer challenges faced by teachers) had higher average achievement scores. A significant part of the achievement gaps between no-fee, fee-paying and independent schools was explained by the type of climate in the school. Also worth noting was that many different dimensions of school climate made a difference. In as much as improving school climate needs to be prioritised, a broad view needs to be adopted when studying the climate of the school. The goal should be to understand how the organisational and professional conditions of the school can support learning. Because the climate of the school will reflect the climate of the community in which it is based, a healthy school climate requires the input and support of school management and the community at large.

8. *Greater expectations endure in spite of the academic difficulties faced by many learners.* While some learners from no-fee schools did not plan to further their education beyond secondary school, there was a high percentage of learners with a low socioeconomic profile who aspired to obtaining an advanced degree. Learners from public schools were also more likely to attend extra lessons, either to excel in class or keep up in class. Further research is needed to understand how extra lessons fit into teaching and learning. It is unclear whether learners attended extra lessons by choice, and whether these lessons were paid for or offered as a service by the community. Because learner support programmes may take many different forms, it is crucial that their quality be regulated and that, wherever possible, learners receive support from accredited organisations. Some would suggest that ambitions for further study are unrealistic, given the many hurdles that these learners will face just to complete secondary school. We take a different view. We would like to believe that an enduring faith in the transformative power of education remains. It is the responsibility of educational leaders to ensure that these hopes are fulfilled.

9. *Continued analyses using local benchmarks should be encouraged to more effectively inform curriculum reform.* We identified 35 per cent of mathematics learners and 28 per cent of science learners in the group of potential learners (scoring between 325 and 400 TIMSS points). With a greater investment, especially in no-fee schools, this group could improve their scores to over 400. The Rasch analysis created national proficiency benchmarks based on South Africa's learner performance. This provided a better sense of the specific competency levels that exist in South Africa and what learners knew relative to the local curriculum requirements. Most importantly, this process revealed in practical terms what teachers needed to cover to help learners move from one benchmark to another. Policy makers, researchers and practitioners would do well to build on this exercise so that local and international assessments can be better integrated. This is not an easy undertaking, but building the links between local and international studies is crucial for future monitoring purposes.

PART A

MATHEMATICS AND SCIENCE ACHIEVEMENT IN SOUTH AFRICA

Mathematics and science achievement in South Africa

1.   Introduction

TIMSS assesses the quality of mathematics and science education globally. This report presents the findings of the TIMSS 2015 for South Africa with a particular focus on the Grade 9 results. A separate report will discuss the Grade 5 study, which was conducted for the first time in South Africa in 2015. TIMSS is one of the most established studies of educational quality worldwide, providing information on learners and the schooling environment and how these characteristics relate to achievement in mathematics and science. South Africa has taken part in TIMSS since 1995[1]. The purpose of this introduction is to explain the role that international assessments play in educational planning. We will also discuss why mathematics and science education are so important in South Africa's present context before presenting the analytical approach that is used in the remainder of the report.

Apartheid education was devastating for black South Africans. Twenty years ago, efforts to reform the curriculum were a priority. Because the quality of education available to African learners was kept deliberately low, it made sense to ensure that all learners had strong foundations in mathematics and science. It was understood that building from this low base would take time; recent indications are that progress has been made but much more needs to be achieved. At the low end of performance, the percentage of learners achieving above a minimum threshold has slowly risen, but overall performance is still low. At the upper reaches, less than two per cent of South African learners achieve results that are comparable with the highest achievers internationally. This is in spite of access to world-class facilities in some of South Africa's wealthier schools.

One of the major challenges facing the South African education system during the past two decades has been how to raise educational standards while closing gaps in student achievement between historically privileged and disadvantaged groups. Progress has been tracked through local and international assessments. The perspective of the two is quite different. Schools, district, provincial and national departments collect information periodically to check that children in different learning environments are reaching a locally based definition of proficient performance. International assessments, like TIMSS, tend to focus on the strengths and weaknesses of education systems as a whole and to monitor changes over time. Global education rankings have become a popular by-product of international assessments. At times a fixation about which countries are at the top and the tail of the league tables has distracted policy makers from evaluating the successes and challenges of individual systems. Moreover, we have often overlooked how the local and international perspectives can complement one another for maximum benefit to policy makers.

There are many valid explanations for why educational quality has not improved more rapidly across the board. Most can be summarised by the following observations: improvements in access to education have not been matched by improvements in quality. Learners come from different home environments and attend schools of varying quality. Learners with fewer socioeconomic resources attend the least-resourced schools and these schools also face organisational challenges. These factors jointly influence the quality of learner outcomes and make it difficult for many learners to achieve even minimum levels of proficiency.

In spite of the past, or perhaps because of it, there is a pressing need to shift the focus away from minimum proficiency and towards raising academic standards in a systematic way. To be sure, a basic understanding of the curriculum remains an important reference point given the country's educational history; but without greater clarity about how to achieve substantial improvements, quality remains low and inequalities persist.

---

[1] South Africa has participated in TIMSS 1995, 1999, 2003, 2011 and 2015.

One of the major challenges facing the South African education system during the past two decades has been how to raise educational standards while closing gaps in student achievement between historically privileged and disadvantaged groups.

1.1. Why mathematics and science are so important in the South African context

Training in mathematics and science is increasingly rewarded in the world of work (CHEC, 2013; Mouton, Boshoff, James & Treptow, 2010; Reddy, Bhorat, Powell, Visser & Arends, 2016b) as the demand for low-skilled labour is rapidly declining (Banerjee, Galiani, Levinsohn, McLaren & Woolard, 2009). High performance standards can also improve the country's global competitiveness (Hanushek & Woessmann, 2015). While we recognise that some learners have a greater innate ability to learn mathematics and science, we also maintain that all learners can benefit from learning these subjects to the best of their ability (PISA, 2016). Exposure to mathematics and science has significant benefits beyond employment opportunities. Mathematics and science improve critical thinking, refine problem-solving abilities and develop abstract reasoning.

A decision about whether to study mathematics and science, and to what level, will have a long-term effect on a learner's life. This makes it all the more important to develop the talents of every learner in these subject areas, regardless of background. To illustrate the extent to which proficiency in mathematics determines future career choices, Figure 1.1 summarises the minimum mathematics entry requirements for entry into a range of science, technology, engineering and mathematics (STEM) degree and diploma programmes offered at South African institutions. The figure summarises the secondary school mathematics requirements to obtain a National Certificate Vocational (NCV)[2] and National Accredited Technical Education Diploma (NATED)[3]. Also shown are National Senior Certificate (NSC)[4] mathematics results required for admission to tertiary certificates, diplomas and degrees. Many certificates, diplomas and degrees at universities and universities of technology require learners to pass mathematics with marks ranging from 30 per cent to 70 per cent, with some degrees needing higher pass rates in mathematics. This list includes interdisciplinary subjects such as agriculture, business science, nursing and architecture that are not traditionally viewed as STEM careers. The point here is that learners should be given the opportunity to develop to their full academic potential, particularly in gatekeeper subjects like mathematics and science.

---

[2] A three-year qualification that is offered at levels 2, 3 and 4 of the National Qualifications Framework (NQF). It is equivalent to Grades 10, 11 and 12.

[3] National Accredited Technical Education Diploma (NATED) programmes that consist of a combination of theoretical study and practical workplace experience.

[4] The National Senior Certificate (NSC) is South Africa's secondary school-leaving examination.

Mathematics and science achievement in South Africa

Figure 1.1: Minimum mathematics requirements for post-school programmes

Mathematics requirements for post-school programmes

Certificates
(Minimum mathematics requirement to obtain admission in a National Certificate Vocational (NCV) and National Accredited Technical Education Diploma (NATED) (Note: NATED indicated in brackets)

Secondary school mathematics requirements	Science/Mathematics Department	Technology Department	Engineering Department
Grade 9	Primary Agriculture	IT and Computer Science	Building Construction; Engineering and related design
Grade 10	Health		Automotive Repair; Civil Engineering; Engineering Fabrication; Renewal Energy and Technology
Grade 11	Systems Development		Chemical Engineering; Civil Engineering; Electrical Engineering; Mechanical Engineering (NATED)
National Senior Certificate (<30%)	Agriculture	Computer Technical Support; Systems Support and Systems Engineering; Database Admin and Database Development	Building Construction; Civil Engineering; Mechanical Engineering (NATED)

Tertiary Certificates, Diplomas and Degrees
(Minimum mathematics requirement to obtain admission to a higher education institutions i.e. University, University of Technology) (Key: ML – Maths Literacy)

National Senior Certificate mathematics achievement	Science/Mathematics	Technology	Engineering
30 – 39%	*Diplomas* Dental assisting		
40 – 49%	*Certificates* Para-medical; *Diplomas* Agriculture; Consumer Science; Food and Nutrition; Dental Technology; Environmental Management; *Degrees* Nursing Science; Sports Science (ML); Audiology; Augmented Life Science/Physical Science; Dental Therapy; Occupational Therapy; Speech Language Therapy	*Certificates* Information and Communication Technology	
50 – 59%	*Diplomas* Analytical chemistry; Biomedical Technology; Biotechnology; Medical Laboratory Sciences; Marine Science; Mathematical Science; *Degrees* Nursing (ML); Agriculture; Applied Chemistry; Biochemistry; Biological Sciences; Biotechnology; Chiropractic; Clinical medical practice; Dietetics; Environmental Earth Science; Genetics; Geography; Geological Sciences; Health Sciences; Microbiology; Nutrition; Optometry; Pharmacy; Physiotherapy; Radiography; Veterinary Nursing	*Degrees* ICT; Information Technology	*Diplomas* Architectural Technology
60 – 69%	*Diplomas* Environmental Management; Landscape Architecture; Socio Informatics; ICT; Information Technology (ML); *Degrees* Biokinetics; Biomedical Sciences; Chemistry; Dental Surgery; Econology; Geographical and Archaeological Sciences; Geology; Human Physiology; Medical Science; Medical and Surgery; Physical Sciences; Plant Science; Veterinary Science; Zoology. Mathematics, Physics, Computer Science and Statistics; Operations Research; Science (General); Statistics	*Degrees* Computer Science; Pulp and Paper Technology	*Diplomas* Clothing and Textile Technology (ML); Engineering; Natural Science; *Degrees* Architecture; Engineering Access Programme; Engineering Technology; Town and Regional Planning; *Degrees* Urban and Regional Planning (ML); Engineering and Environmental Geology; Quantity Surveying; Maritime Studies; Natural Science; Surveying
70 – 79%	*Degrees* Astronomy and Astrophysics; Business Science; Econometrics; Mathematics Statistics; Mathematics; Nuclear Science and Engineering		
80 – 100%	*Degrees* Actuarial and Financial Mathematics		

Source: Central Applications Office, 2017

PART A

Policy makers recognise that the number of learners achieving quality passes in mathematics needs to increase. The Medium Term Strategic Framework (MTSF) includes Grade 12 mathematics results among its impact indicators for quality basic education (DPME, 2014). There are some signs of improvement: it is estimated, for example, that the number of better-performing black students increased between 2008 and 2015 (Gustafsson, 2016). This upward trend opens a number of doors for STEM and health-related tertiary courses but as Figure 1.2 shows, mathematics and science results continue to lag behind other subject areas. The percentage of learners that achieved a pass rate of 40 per cent or higher in mathematics and physical science was considerably lower than for other subjects such as history, geography and business studies. Only 34 per cent of full-time candidates achieved 40 per cent or higher in mathematics in 2016, compared to 64 per cent of candidates who wrote history and 50 per cent who wrote business studies.

Figure 1.2: Percentage of candidates achieving 40 per cent and above in a selection of NSC subjects, 2015 and 2016

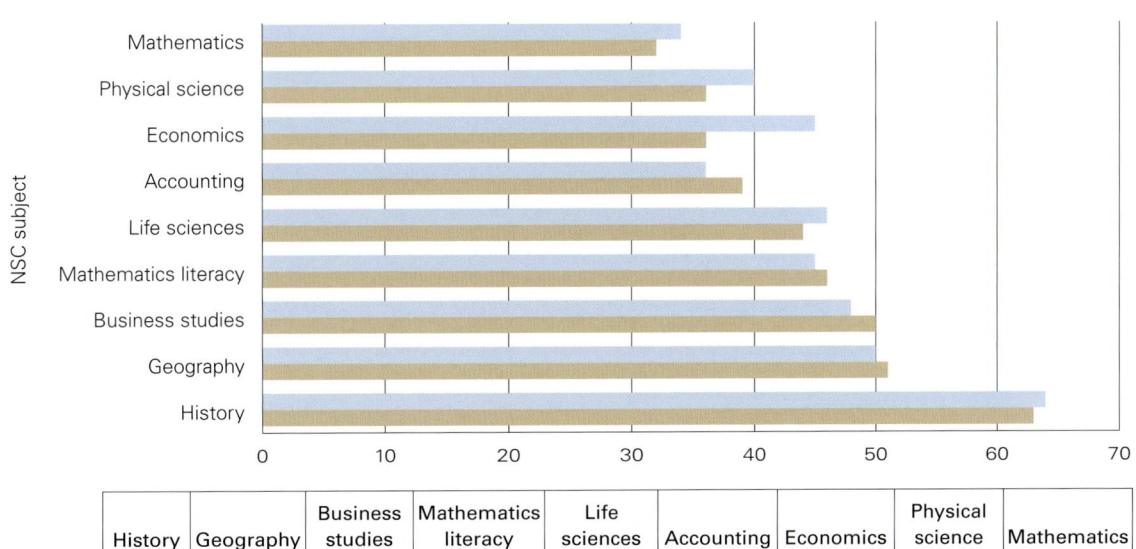

	History	Geography	Business studies	Mathematics literacy	Life sciences	Accounting	Economics	Physical science	Mathematics
2016	64	50	48	45	46	36	45	40	34
2015	63	51	50	46	44	39	36	36	32

Source: DBE, 2016b

Improving the quality and consistency of mathematics and science education will certainly not resolve all the post-schooling challenges facing learners, but it will surely increase the chances of learners completing secondary school with better opportunities in STEM fields. This will, in turn, expand access to a wider range of post-school education and training programmes beyond secondary school, and ultimately improve job prospects. There are consequences for society as a whole and for economic development when learners' choices are severely constrained.

1.2. National educational policies and practices

Great strides have been made in education legislation, policy development and curriculum reform over the past 20 years. In the 1990s, the White Paper on Education and Training (DoE, 1995), the National Education Policy Act (No. 27 of 1996) and the South African Schools Act (No. 84 of 1996) focused on addressing past inequalities in the South African education system. From the early 2000s, policy reforms have continued to focus on closing historical gaps in education delivery (DBE, 2011b; DoE, 2001b). The National Development Plan (NDP) to 2030 asserts that building national capabilities requires quality early childhood development, basic education, further and higher education (National Planning Commission, 2011). The priorities in basic education, as noted in the NDP, are human capacity, school management, district support, infrastructure and results-oriented mutual accountability between schools and communities. Globally, South Africa has adopted the United Nations' Sustainable Development Goals (SDGs) (United Nations, 2017). Efforts have been made to align the fourth SDG, on inclusive and equitable quality education and the promotion of lifelong learning opportunities for all, with the education goals of the NDP.

Mathematics and science achievement in South Africa

Certain policies, such as the National Strategy for Mathematics, Science and Technology Education (NSMSTE), have specifically targeted improvements in mathematics, science and technology education (DoE, 2001a). National policies have sometimes referred to pass rates in mathematics and science and to South Africa's performance in international assessments (DPME, 2014). The TIMSS results are mentioned in the Action Plan to 2014, with a target set at 420 average score points in TIMSS mathematics by 2023 (DBE, 2011a). Below, we provide a brief synopsis of policies and structures that are most relevant to the framework of this report.

Gender

The purpose of the Gender Equity unit within the DBE is to advise the Director-General (DG) on different aspects of gender equity in the education system. Advice to the DG includes: the correction of gender imbalances in enrolment, dropouts, subject choice, career paths and performance; guidelines to address sexism in curricula, textbooks, teaching and guidance; and a strategy to counter and eliminate sexism, sexual harassment and gender violence throughout the education system (Commission for Gender Equality, 2007; DBE, 2017a).

Language of learning and teaching (LoLT)

South African policy documents state that learners have the right to education in their home language, but the school language policy is determined by the School Governing Body (SGB) of the school (Basic Education Laws Amendment Act [No. 15 of 2011]; South African Constitution, 1998). When the home and teaching language are not the same, then the academic development of learners can be affected. The Incremental Introduction of African Languages (IIAL) policy is intended to promote and develop the use of previously marginalised African languages in schools so that learners can access languages other than English and Afrikaans (DBE, 2013b). The IIAL policy will be introduced in phases, commencing in Grade 1 in 2015 and continuing until 2026 when it will be implemented in Grade 12.

Learning and teaching support material (LTSM)

The Draft National Policy for the Provision and Management of Learning and Teaching Support Material (LTSM) provides guidelines for the development, selection, procurement and utilisation of quality LTSM, which includes stationery and supplies, learning material, teaching aids and science, technology, mathematics and biology apparatus (DBE, 2014). Every learner and teacher should have access to the minimum set of core materials required to implement the curriculum. Textbooks, workbooks and teacher guides are considered as core LTSMs because they are considered essential for covering the curriculum as stated in the Action Plan to 2019, Goal 19 (DBE, 2015a).

School infrastructure

Perhaps the most obvious forms of inequality are those that relate to infrastructure, basic services, equipment and furniture. In addressing these discrepancies, the DBE published the National Policy for an Equitable Provision of an Enabling School Physical Teaching and Learning Environment (DBE, 2010); Guidelines Relating to Planning for Public School Infrastructure (DBE, 2012a); and the School Infrastructure Safety and Security Guidelines (DBE, 2017b). Based on the Guidelines Relating to Planning for Public School Infrastructure, the environment of a school is graded according to: basic safety, minimum functionality, optimum functionality, and enrichment. The DBE established the Accelerated Schools Infrastructure Development Initiative, which is a programme to build schools across the country, with a large focus on addressing backlogs in school infrastructure and providing basic services to schools.

Libraries and information services

It is crucial to provide access to credible and high-quality library and information services in support of curriculum implementation. The DBE therefore developed the National Guidelines for School Library and Information Services in 2012 (DBE, 2012b). The School Library and Information Services at the provincial Departments of Education are expected to collaborate with the DBE for guidance and support regarding infrastructure, staffing, information and communications technology (ICT) usage, basic library management and budgeting, including advice on using a percentage of the LTSM budget for library resources based on the schools' needs. The DBE proposes a wide range of alternatives in providing library and information services, which includes the provision of classroom libraries, cluster, mobile and school community libraries, to a fully-fledged library and information service in all schools (DBE, 2012b).

School safety, bullying, violence

School violence affects all schools, irrespective of location, and therefore all schools are required to develop a school safety policy, with plans and data collection tools to enable them to proactively deal with and better manage threats to school safety (GDE, 2012). The DBE developed a National School Safety Framework to serve as a management tool for provincial and district officials responsible for school safety, principals, senior management team members, SGB members, teachers and learners to identify and manage risk and threats of violence in and around schools, including cyber bullying. The framework is critical to empowering all responsible officials in understanding their responsibilities regarding school safety (DBE, 2015c).

The DBE has furthermore developed a national strategy for the prevention and management of alcohol and drug use among learners in schools; and schools have been provided with a Guide to Drug Testing in South African Schools (DBE, 2013a). In terms of the Regulations for Safety Measures at all Public Schools in the South African Schools Act, the Minister has declared all public schools as drug-free and dangerous weapon-free zones. The DBE has proposed plans to address violence in schools that are intended to train teachers to deal with aggression in the classroom, strengthen relationships between schools and communities and hold school management accountable (DBE, 2015d).

2.   Analytical approach

A considerable amount of thought and effort has gone into resourcing schools, training teachers and improving school leadership in South African schools. However, the impact of interventions and policies has varied. Previous TIMSS reports have confirmed that improvements in mathematics and science outcomes have occurred and achievement gaps have to some extent narrowed. Nonetheless, educational inputs and outputs still remain highly unequal across South African schools (Reddy, Kanjee, Diedericks & Winnaar, 2006; Reddy et al., 2015). Based on the TIMSS international benchmarks, the majority of South African learners were yet to achieve a minimum level of competency as defined by the international component of the study (Mullis, Martin, Foy & Hooper, 2016).

There is another way to look at these results. TIMSS 2015 is the fifth time that South Africa has participated in the Grade 9 study. The current report provides an opportunity to take stock of past results and to reframe our understanding of what is required to raise academic standards. This report builds on the successful use of international studies by using the results to inform local realities in 2015. While rankings and standards will continue to add value to the policy discussion, the complexity of South African learning environments requires thinking differently about these results.

Mathematics and science achievement in South Africa

To maximise the benefit of the TIMSS study for policy makers and practitioners, three approaches will be used to present the 2015 results for South Africa in this report. The first is descriptive. Parts A, B, C and D provide an overview of performance based on where learners lived and learned. This is the traditional approach that we have used in previous reports and it continues to provide valuable insights. We compare mean scores and percentiles among different groups of learners and schooling environments. We also discuss interesting and important developments in non-cognitive factors that are related to achievement, such as learner aspirations, exposure to bullying and the level of academic support outside of school.

Using the data to full potential relies on an understanding of learning conditions within South Africa. One of the innovations of this report is that we include two additional methodological approaches to improve our understanding of what these results mean locally. The second methodological approach is inferential. In Part E, we use multilevel analysis to investigate which combination of factors is associated with TIMSS learner achievement. This requires an analysis of learner characteristics alongside enabling inputs within the school. The third approach is psychometric and is discussed in Part F. National proficiency benchmarks have been developed that are more closely aligned to the South African educational context. IRT is used to compare what learners know to what they are expected to know based on the local curriculum. The process also describes what is needed for learners to reach the next level of proficiency. This new direction will deepen our interpretation of the TIMSS results and what is realistically required for learners to make incremental progress in these crucial subject areas. We present both the mathematics and science results in the descriptive discussions. However, we focus on one of the two subjects in discussing the psychometric and multilevel results and refer readers to full-length reports for additional details. We demonstrate the psychometric approach to developing national benchmarks using the science results and multilevel analysis is based on the mathematics results.

Many South African learners face serious obstacles to learning mathematics and science and the causes are complex. Including a local interpretation of the data in our presentation of the 2015 study permits clearer policy interpretations of how to support specific groups of learners, their teachers and their educational environments. As we will show in this report, poor performance is related to the school, to the learners themselves and to their out-of-school environment. Whatever the root cause, the impact is clear at every educational phase and as young adults transition from school into the workplace. All too often, South African learners face diverging destinies. The key predictor of academic success, particularly in technical subjects, remains where learners happen to live and learn. It is hoped that this report will provide insights that will shift the current path and help to generate new pathways to support higher achievement.

3.   Trends in TIMSS results[5]

The TIMSS 2015 sample for South Africa was drawn from the 2013 DBE master list of all schools in South Africa, which comprised 10 009 schools (9 099 public and 910 independent schools) that offered Grade 9 classes. Statistics Canada drew the South African sample by using the province, school type (public and independent) and LoLT (Afrikaans, English and dual medium) as stratification variables. A total of 300 schools were sampled, of which 292 participated in the study. A total of 12 514 learners, 334 mathematics and 331 science teachers participated in the study. Data from the principal, teacher and learner questionnaires, as well as learner achievement data are used in this report. A full description of the TIMSS 2015 design and methodology is available in Appendix 1. The appendix also explains how the TIMSS conceptual framework guides the study design.

---

[5] The results presented in this section build on the findings that were published in: Highlights of Mathematics and Science Achievement of Grade 9 South African learners (Reddy et al., 2016a).

The traditional TIMSS methodology provides an opportunity for a country to measure change in its own performance over time (Reddy et al., 2016a). In the TIMSS 2011 report we showed that the South African performance for mathematics and science was the same for the 1995, 1999 and 2003 cycles (Reddy et al., 2015). Between TIMSS 2003 and 2011, the mathematics and science scores improved by 67 and 64 points respectively[6]. Between 2011 and 2015 the mathematics and science scores improved by a further 20 and 26 points respectively.

3.1 Trends in performance percentiles

There are two important findings based on the trend analysis of TIMSS performance from 2003 to 2015. Figure 3.1 summarises South African performance by different percentiles for TIMSS 2003, 2011 and 2015 for both mathematics and science. First, the highest gains were achieved at the lower end of the achievement distribution, which means that those with the lowest levels of achievement are improving. The second is based on the overall shape and size of the achievement distribution. The longer the line, the wider the variation in scores, which, in turn, suggests large educational inequalities among learners. The distribution of scores is still wide, but has narrowed from 2003 to 2011, and again to 2015, showing a narrowing of the gap between the top and the bottom performers. This is true for both mathematics and science but the change has been greater for mathematics.

Figure 3.1: National trends in Grade 9 mathematics and science achievement, 2003, 2011 and 2015 (with SEs)[a]

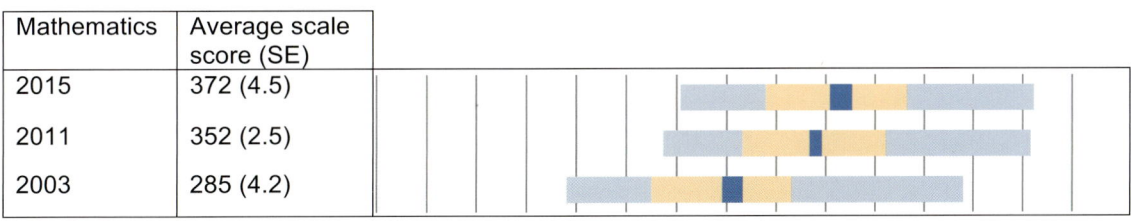

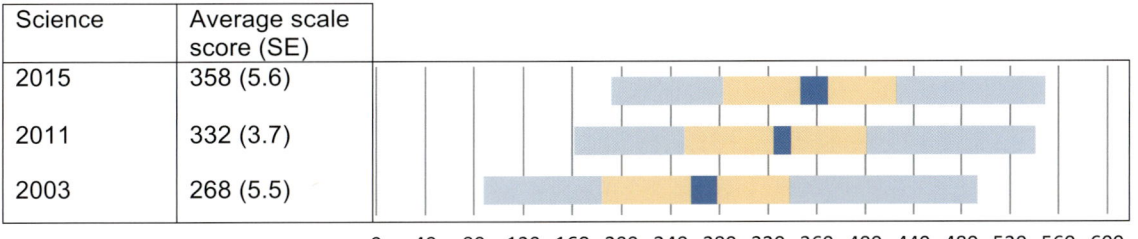

[a] TIMSS 2003 tested both Grade 8 and Grade 9 learners. Results reported in Figure 3.1 are based on Grade 9 learner performance.

---

[6] TIMSS estimates that an improvement of 40 TIMSS points over a four-year cycle is equivalent to an improvement of one grade. South Africa did not participate in the TIMSS 2007 study. Therefore, over an eight-year cycle (from 2003 to 2011), South African national performance corresponded to 1.5 grades.

Mathematics and science achievement in South Africa

3.2   Change in performance from 2003 to 2015

In Figure 3.2, changes in national scores are compared across a selection of 25 countries that participated in TIMSS 2003 and TIMSS 2015, including South Africa. Bars to the right in Figure 3.2 show the improvement in scores between TIMSS 2003 and TIMSS 2015, and bars to the left show a decrease in scores. The length of the bar represents the amount by which the country score has changed. Of the 25 countries included in the analysis, 19 experienced an improvement in mathematics scores between the two cycles and five a decline. For science, there was a decline in the achievement scores of 12 countries. South Africa has shown the biggest positive change, with an improvement of 90 points in science and 87 points in mathematics. This upward shift translates to an overall performance improvement of approximately two grade levels between 2003 and 2015. Granted, this increase was from a very low base but it still underscores the substantial improvement that took place during this period, where many other countries showed little change or even negative trends.

Figure 3.2: Change in average mathematics and science scores of selected countries, 2003 and 2015

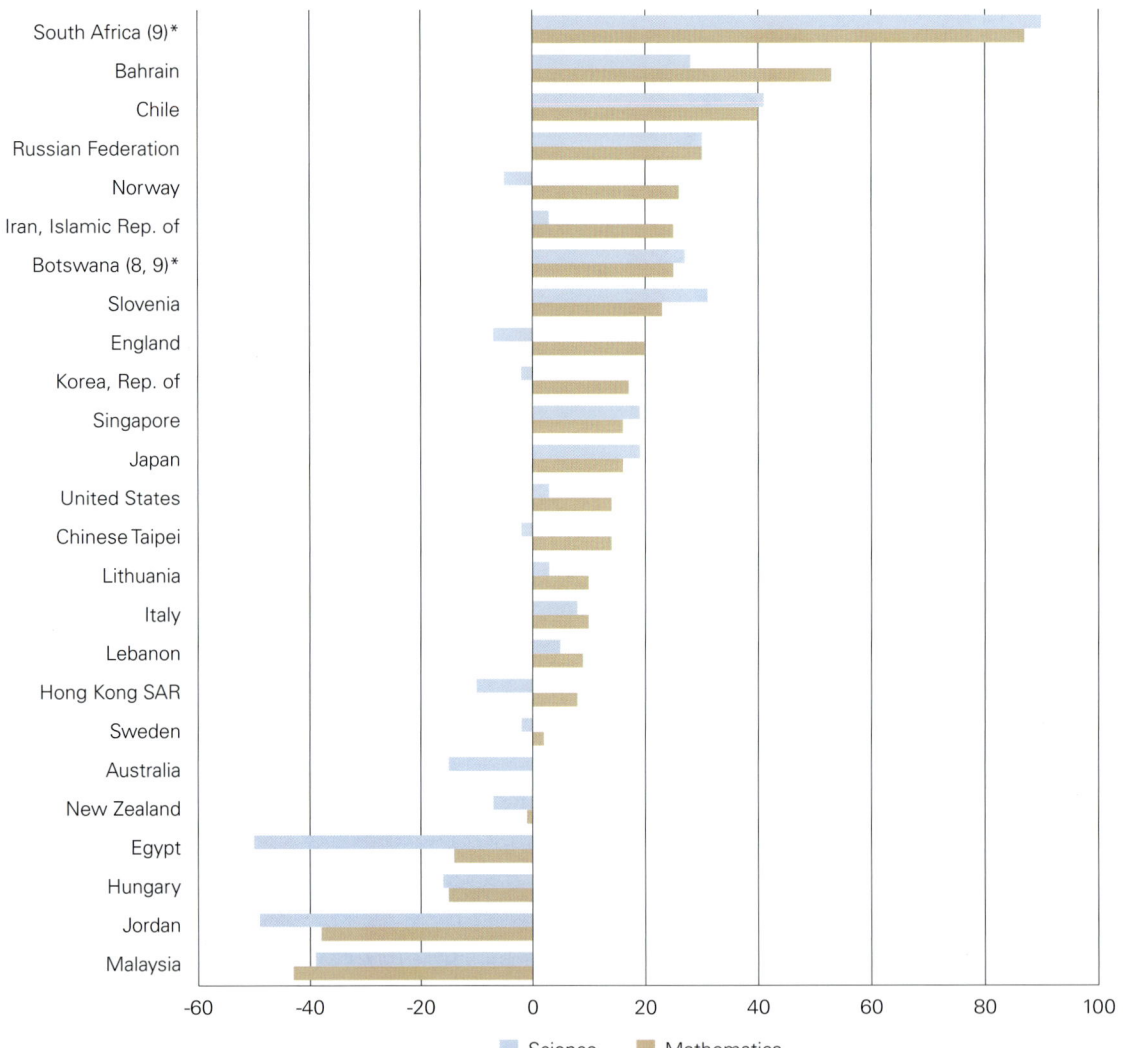

*Grade tested

PART A

TIMSS International has created a set of international benchmarks to provide participating countries with comparable descriptions of what learners know. TIMSS defines four categories of benchmarks, namely: scores between 400 and 475 points are classified as achievement at a *low* level, scores between 475 and 550 points as achievement at an *intermediate* level, scores from 550 to 625 points as achievement at a *high* level and scores above 625 points as achievement at an *advanced* level. Table 3.1 below provides a brief description of what the different benchmarks represent.

Table 3.1: Description of TIMSS international benchmarks, 2015

Benchmark	Descriptions for mathematics	Descriptions for sciences
Low	Have some knowledge of whole numbers and basic graphs	Learners show some basic knowledge of biology, chemistry, physics and earth science
Intermediate	Can apply basic mathematical knowledge in a variety of situations	Learners demonstrate and apply their knowledge of biology, chemistry, physics and earth science in various contexts
High	Can apply understanding and knowledge in a variety of relatively complex situations	Learners apply and communicate understanding of concepts from biology, chemistry, physics and earth science in everyday and abstract situations
Advanced	Can apply and reason in a variety of problem situations, solve linear equations, and make generalisations	Learners communicate understanding of complex concepts related to biology, chemistry, physics and earth science in practical, abstract, and experimental contexts

Source: (Mullis et al., 2016)

To provide a more textured picture of South African performance, we have included a fifth South African category. The fifth category refers to the percentage of learners who achieved between 325 and 400 score points. We call this group the potential group, as these learners have the potential to improve their scores to above 400 points. Figure 3.3 illustrates the South African profile at the different TIMSS benchmarks (including the South African potential group) for mathematics and science for 2003, 2011 and 2015.

In 2015, 34 per cent of mathematics learners and 32 per cent of science learners achieved a score of over 400-points. This means that only one-third of South African Grade 9 learners demonstrated achievement at the minimal level in mathematics and science. The encouraging news is that 3.2 per cent of mathematics learners and 4.9 per cent of science learners can be categorised at the high levels of achievement (i.e. scoring over 550).

Figure 3.3 also shows the change in the percentage of South African learners who performed above the 400-point TIMSS benchmark for mathematics and science between 2003 and 2015. In 2003, only 10.5 per cent of mathematics learners achieved a score above 400 points. This increased to 24.5 per cent in 2011 and to 34.3 per cent in 2015. Therefore, between 2003 and 2015 there was an increase of 24 percentage points in the number of learners scoring above 400. Science scores followed a similar pattern. In 2003, 13.1 per cent of science learners achieved a score of over 400. This percentage increased to 25.2 per cent in 2011 and to 32.3 per cent in 2015. Between 2003 and 2015 there was an increase of 19 percentage points.

It is also worth pointing out the changes in the proportion of learners scoring below 325 points (a nationally defined benchmark). In 2003, 73 per cent of Grade 9 mathematics learners and 72 per cent of Grade 9 science learners scored below 325 points. This has decreased to 31 per cent of mathematics learners and 40 per cent of science learners in 2015. Performance in mathematics and science appears to have shifted from a very low level to a low level.

Mathematics and science achievement in South Africa

Figure 3.3: Percentage of learners performing at the TIMSS international benchmarks, 2003, 2011 and 2015

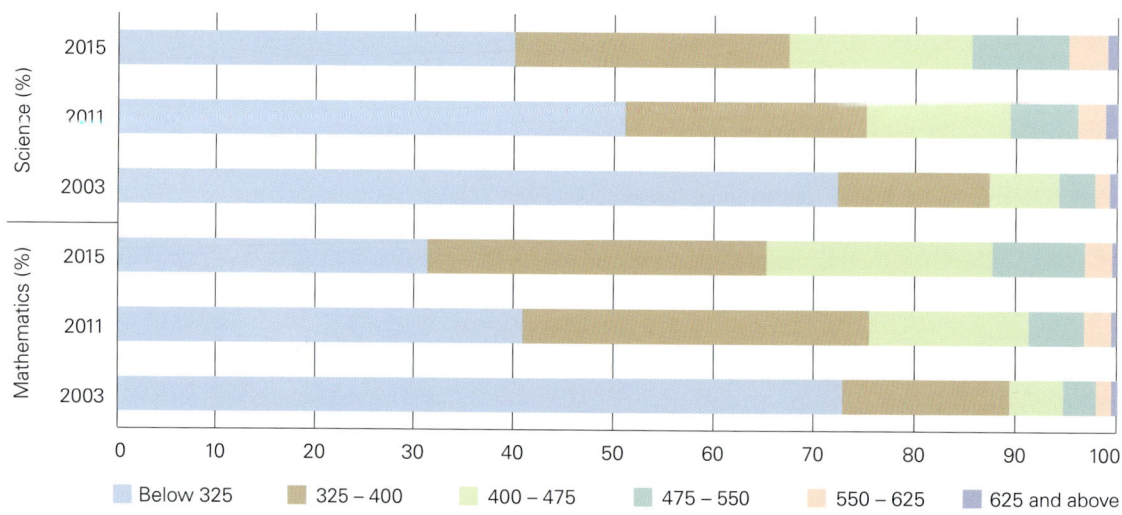

3.3   Provincial performance

In South Africa, the national DBE shares responsibility for basic schooling with provincial departments, as it is the task of each provincial department to finance and manage its schools directly. Given the responsibilities of the provincial departments of education, it is useful to report on provincial performance. TIMSS oversampled the number of schools and learners so that reliable estimates of provincial performance could be provided. The TIMSS 2015 provincial mathematics and science performance is shown in Figure 3.4 below.

The ranking order of the provinces for TIMSS 2015 mathematics with Standard Errors (SE) was: Gauteng (GT) with a score of 408 (SE 11.4), Western Cape (WC) 391(SE 11.0), Mpumalanga (MP) 370 (SE 7.8), KwaZulu-Natal (KZ) 369 (SE 11.8), Free State (FS) 367 (SE 12.5), Northern Cape (NC) 364 (SE 7.2), Limpopo (LP) 361 (SE 13.4), North West (NW) 354 (SE 7.9), and Eastern Cape (EC) 346 (SE 14.4).

The ranking order of the provinces for TIMSS 2015 science was: GT with a score of 405 (SE 13.8), WC 388 (SE 12.7), NC 356 (SE 8.9), KZ 352 (SE 14.7), FS 351 (SE 15.3), MP 348 (SE 9.6), LP 339 (SE 15.8), NW 335 (SE 10.0), and EC 328 (SE 17.6).

Figure 3.4: Provincial mathematics and science performance with 95 per cent confidence intervals, 2015

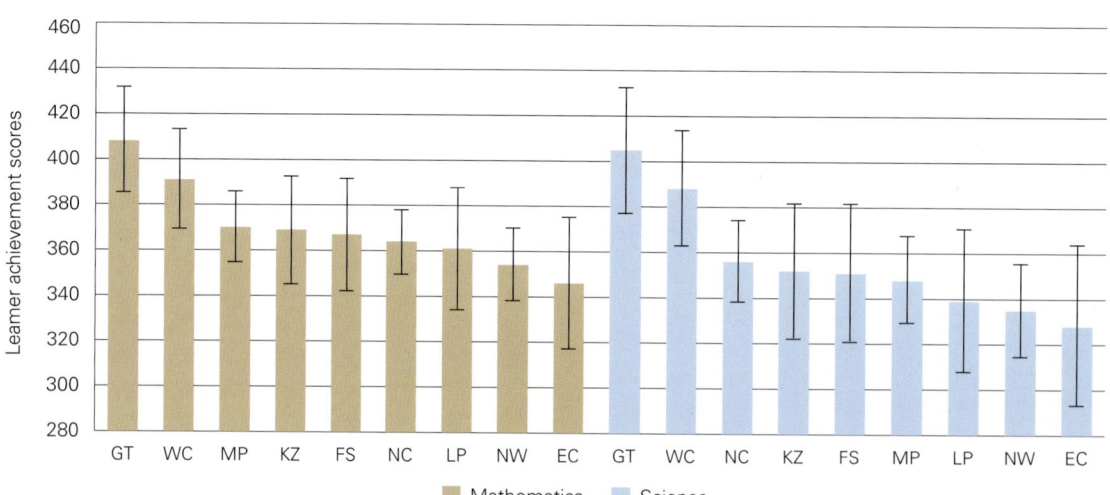

The increase in the national average mathematics and science scores from TIMSS 2003 to TIMSS 2011 to TIMSS 2015 is reflected by an increase in the scores of most provinces. The change in mathematics and science performance from TIMSS 2003 to TIMSS 2015 is shown in Figure 3.5. In 2003, the difference in performance between the highest- and lowest-performing provinces was 170 points for mathematics and 205 points for science. This difference decreased in 2011, to 88 points for mathematics and 127 points for science. In 2015, the difference decreased further to 62 points for mathematics and 77 points for science. This improvement by the lower-performing provinces points to a move towards more equitable achievement across the provinces. Since 2003, the average scale score has increased in eight provinces for mathematics and seven provinces for science. Limpopo has shown the highest average score increase in mathematics and science, namely 117 points and 123 points, respectively. In later sections, we see how the profile of learners and schools has changed, which could provide an explanation for the changes in the performance of the provinces.

Figure 3.5: Difference in provincial performance in mathematics and science, 2003 and 2015

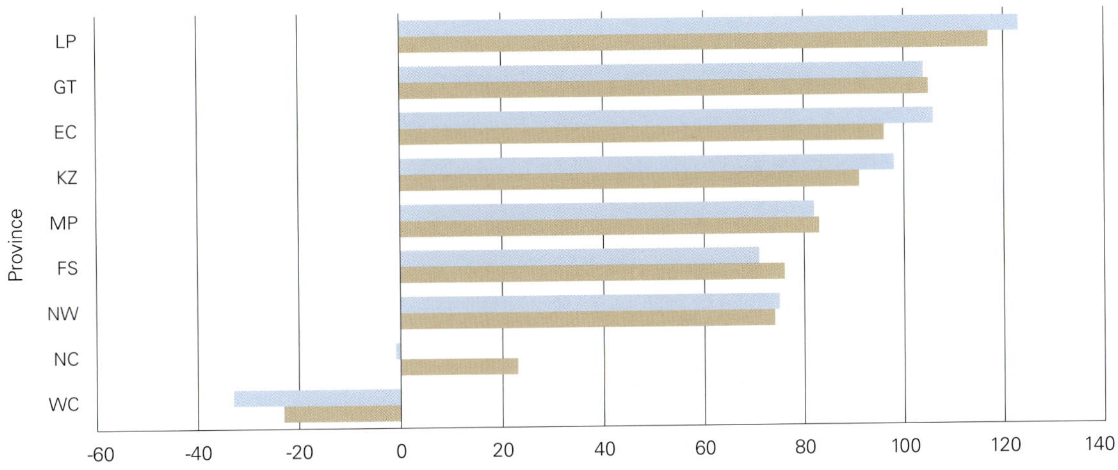

	WC	NC	NW	FS	MP	KZ	EC	GT	LP
Science	-33	-1	75	71	82	98	106	104	123
Mathematics	-23	23	74	76	83	91	96	105	117

3.4   Performance by school type

The South African schooling system consists of public schools, independent schools, special schools and Early Childhood Development (ECD) sites. Whereas 92.7 per cent of learners attend public schools, only 4.1 per cent are in independent schools (DBE, 2016a). There are marked differences in the physical conditions of South African schools depending on the contexts in which they are located. These differences are captured by the poverty index of schools (quintile ranking 1 to 5). As part of the government's pro-poor strategy to support education, schools in quintiles 1, 2 and 3 receive subsidies that make it possible to exempt learners from paying fees. Thus, public schools are differentiated into fee-paying schools and no-fee schools. Of the learners who participated in TIMSS 2015, 65 per cent attended no-fee schools, 31 per cent fee-paying schools and four per cent independent schools.

Figure 3.6 on page 26 shows the average learner scores in mathematics and science for learners in the three school types for TIMSS 2011 and TIMSS 2015. The average mathematics and science scores for each of the school types are significantly different, with no-fee schools recording the lowest performance. In TIMSS 2015, the average mathematics scores and SEs for the different school types are: no-fee schools 341 (SE 3.3) points, fee-paying schools 423 (SE 10.0) and independent schools 477 (SE 11.5). For science the average scores are: no-fee schools 317 (SE 4.2), fee-paying schools 425 (SE 11.9) and independent schools 485 (SE 11.8).

Mathematics and science achievement in South Africa

Figure 3.6 also shows how the increases in TIMSS scores from 2011 to 2015 play out differently across the different school types, with learners in public schools achieving the largest gains. The achievement scores of learners who attended no-fee schools increased by 17 and 23 points for mathematics and science, respectively. Learners who attended fee-paying schools increased their scores by 26 and 31 points for mathematics and science, respectively. Learners who attended independent schools only increased their scores by 4 and 6 points for mathematics and science, respectively.

The average scores of the more affluent school types (the independent and the fee-paying schools) did not reach the TIMSS international centre point score of 500 in spite of the better resources in many of these environments. The gap between the average mathematics performance of fee-paying and independent schools narrowed from three-quarters of a standard deviation in 2011 to half a standard deviation in 2015. The gap between fee-paying and no-fee schools remained at three-quarters of a standard deviation for mathematics and one standard deviation for science.

Figure 3.6: Average performance by school type, 2011 and 2015

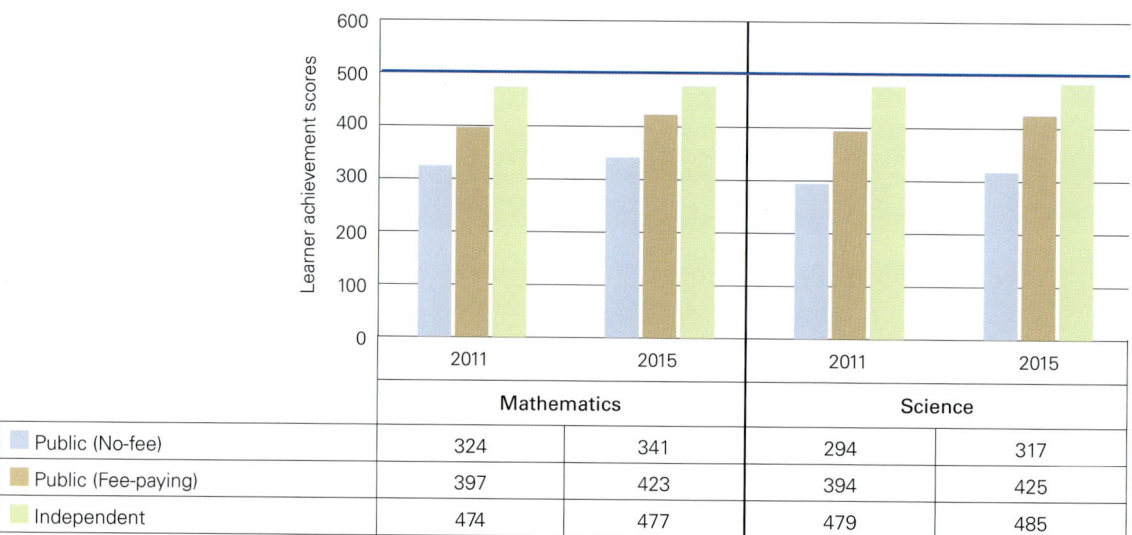

	Mathematics		Science	
	2011	2015	2011	2015
Public (No-fee)	324	341	294	317
Public (Fee-paying)	397	423	394	425
Independent	474	477	479	485

Section summary

The need to improve mathematics and science skills among South Africans continues. A wide range of post-schooling opportunities require foundations in mathematics and science and policy makers recognise the need for quality passes in mathematics and science. The NSC results show that the percentage of learners passing mathematics and science is lower than that of other key subjects. There have been some important gains over time, particularly among learners in the poorest-performing provinces and the least-resourced schools. The gap between high and low achievers has also narrowed. However, average scores for learners in no-fee schools remain far below the TIMSS international centre point of 500 for all countries. Even in fee-paying and independent schools, average scores are yet to reach the scale centre point of 500. When the results of learner home environments are compared, some important policy insights emerge.

PART **B**

LEARNERS AND THE HOME ENVIRONMENT

Learners and the home environment

There are many ways in which a learner's background and home environment is related to academic outcomes.

This section focuses on the relationship between learner characteristics, the home environment and TIMSS Grade 9 mathematics and science outcomes. There are many ways in which a learner's background and home environment is related to academic outcomes. Sometimes this is because children are treated differently by family members depending on their age, gender and the strength of cultural expectations (Lubienski, Robinson, Crane & Ganley, 2013). Older children are more likely to have repeated a grade level. They may also have more responsibilities at home than younger children, leaving less time available for schoolwork. The relationship between gender and academic outcomes has been somewhat mixed in South Africa but gender gaps in achievement that favour boys have been narrowing (Zuze et al., 2015). There is a positive relationship between the socioeconomic resources in the home and academic outcomes (Taylor & Yu, 2009). Better-educated parents are more likely to be employed, which means that their children have additional resources to support success at school (Branson, Lam & Zuze, 2012; Case & Deaton, 1999; Fleisch, 2008). Parents with fewer socioeconomic resources can also support their children academically but they face more challenges in doing so (Harris & Robinson, 2016). Levels of poverty remain high in South Africa. Over 12 million child support grants are distributed each month (SASSA, 2017). Families grapple on a daily basis with how to meet their children's basic needs. In this environment of scarcity there is a limit to the educational resources that learners can access outside of school.

4. A profile of Grade 9 learners in 2015

4.1 Gender, age and achievement

In Figure 4.1, the age distribution of learners is compared across schooling environments. It is based on age at the time of the TIMSS test administration in August 2015. Grade 9 learners who started school at the correct age, and who progressed through school without repeating a grade or other interruptions, would have been aged between 13.5 and 15.0 years at the start of the academic year in January and would be between 14.0 and 15.5 years in the middle of the academic year (Education Laws Amendment Act No. 50 of 2002). At a national level, 51 per cent of Grade 9 learners are age appropriate. The majority of over-aged learners were in the public school system. In 2015, 43 per cent of Grade 9 learners in no-fee schools were age appropriate for their grade compared to 64 per cent of learners in fee-paying schools and 73 per cent of learners in independent schools.

Figure 4.1: Age distribution by school type, 2015

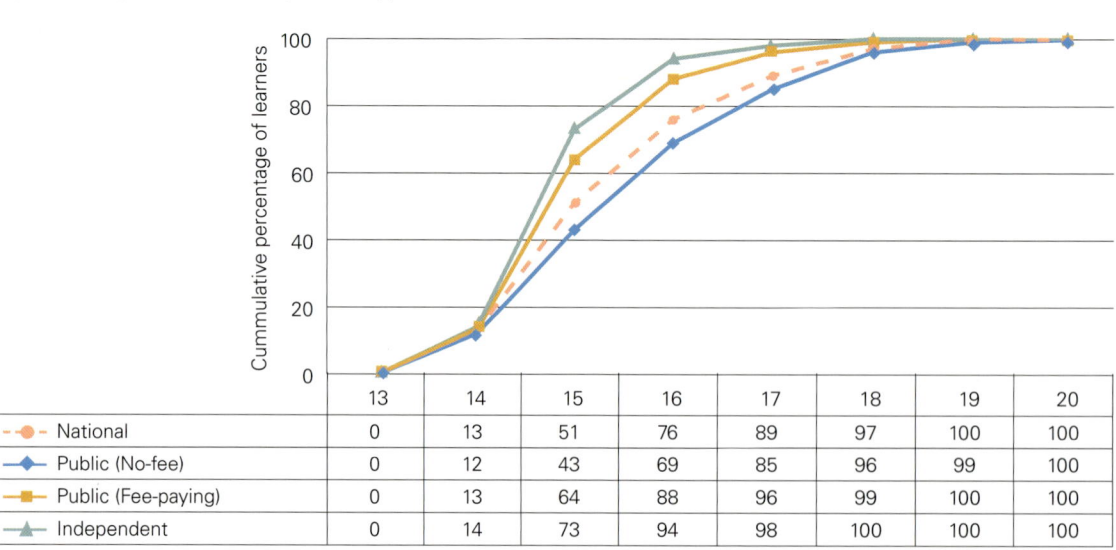

	13	14	15	16	17	18	19	20
National	0	13	51	76	89	97	100	100
Public (No-fee)	0	12	43	69	85	96	99	100
Public (Fee-paying)	0	13	64	88	96	99	100	100
Independent	0	14	73	94	98	100	100	100

Figure 4.2 compares average achievement scores by age for girls and boys at the time of the TIMSS study in August 2015. In 2011, boys who were age appropriate for their grade significantly outperformed girls in mathematics and science (Reddy et al., 2015). In contrast, there were no gender differences in achievement for age-appropriate learners in 2015. Although there were no statistically significant age-based gender differences, older girls achieved lower average test scores than older boys. It is important to point out the effect that dropping out will have on the pool of boys and girls remaining in school. As early as Grade 6, dropout rates are higher among boys than among girls and the gap increases each year (Branson & Hofmeyer, 2013). If boys who dropout are weaker learners, then an academically stronger group of boys is being compared to a more academically mixed group of girls.

Figure 4.2: Average achievement scores by age and gender, 2015

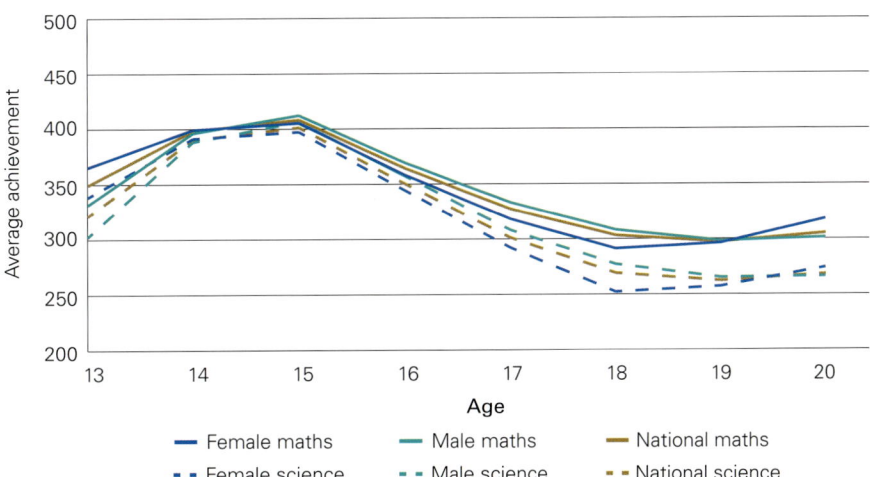

4.2   Language of learning and teaching (LoLT)

In any multilingual society, language plays an important and often complex role in teaching and learning. South Africa is no exception to this rule (Setati & Adler, 2000). Lack of language proficiency is known to be one of the reasons for poor performance in local and international assessments. The IIAL policy has been introduced to expand the use of and access to African languages in schools in phases, beginning in 2015 (DBE, 2013b). Language experts continue to discover innovative ways to use language effectively to support mathematics and science instruction. Using more than one language in the classroom is one popular example, but there are differences in how consistently and effectively these methods have been applied (Adler, 1998; Probyn, 2009). Teachers must strike a fine balance between helping their learners to grasp mathematical concepts in a language other than the official one and exposing them to mathematical English or Afrikaans for assessment purposes (Adler, 1999, 2006). Learners who are fluent in the language of instruction and who are regularly exposed to this language outside of school operate outside these confines and are at an advantage.

The TIMSS assessment is administered in either English or Afrikaans, depending on the language policy of the school. Grade 9 learners were asked how frequently they used the language of the TIMSS assessment outside of school. In Table 4.1, trends and average achievement are compared. Nationally, the percentage of learners speaking the test language either 'always' or 'almost always' increased by six percentage points between 2003 and 2015. Average achievement in both mathematics and science was significantly higher for learners with greater fluency in the test language. Language plays an important role in academic performance. As we will discuss in Parts E and F, part of the importance of language is because it increases the difficulties already faced by vulnerable learners.

Learners and the home environment

Table 4.1: Average achievement by frequency of speaking the test language, 2003, 2011 and 2015

	Always or almost always		Sometimes		Never	
	% learners (SE)	Average achievement (SE)	% learners (SE)	Average achievement (SE)	% learners (SE)	Average achievement (SE)
Mathematics 2003	25 (1.7)	358 (9.1)	64 (1.7)	269 (3.0)	12 (0.8)	226 (6.2)
Mathematics 2011	26 (1.0)	405 (4.5)	65 (1.2)	337 (2.2)	9 (0.6)	312 (4.9)
Mathematics 2015	31 (1.6)	416 (6.2)	63 (1.5)	356 (4.1)	6 (0.4)	325 (5.6)
Science 2003	25 (1.7)	359 (10.9)	64 (1.7)	248 (4.6)	12 (0.8)	192 (6.7)
Science 2011	26 (1.0)	412 (5.9)	65 (1.2)	310 (3.4)	9 (0.6)	264 (6.1)
Science 2015	31 (1.6)	419 (7.3)	63 (1.5)	335 (4.9)	6 (0.4)	295 (6.9)

In Table 4.2, this relationship is compared to assessment results in different school groupings. As one would expect, within both public and independent schools, learners who spoke the language of the test either 'always' or 'almost always' achieved better average test scores and learners who never spoke the language of the test outside school had the lowest test scores. Within the same schooling category, the average achievement gap based on frequency of speaking the test language was wider for science than for mathematics. For example, in independent schools the gap was 72 points for mathematics and 84 points for science, while in fee-paying schools it was 76 points and 101 points respectively. Similarly, in no-fee schools the gap was 46 points for mathematics and 70 points for science. These results make sense because the science curriculum relies more on reading and writing than mathematics, where problem solving can be expressed in non-written formats.

Table 4.2: Average achievement by frequency of speaking the test language and school type, 2015

School type	Frequency of speaking test language	Average mathematics achievement (SE)	Average science achievement (SE)
Independent	Always or almost always	508 (13.7)	522 (12.2)
	Sometimes	437 (11.5)	436 (12.9)
	Never	437 (23.3)	438 (23.7)
Public (Fee-paying)	Always or almost always	448 (8.6)	459 (9.7)
	Sometimes	400 (11.8)	392 (14.0)
	Never	371 (16.8)	358 (18.1)
Public (No-fee)	Always or almost always	357 (4.6)	346 (6.2)
	Sometimes	340 (3.4)	314 (4.2)
	Never	311 (5.5)	276 (7.2)

5. Home resources

Public expenditure on education has focused on reversing historical deficits in resource distribution in schools (Gustafsson & Patel, 2006). National poverty alleviation programmes also play an important role in keeping children in school. The National School Nutrition Programme (NSNP) is active in over 19 000 no-fee schools (DBE, 2015b). The expansion of age eligibility for the child support grant has improved the chances of learners aged between 15 and 19 enrolling in school, at a critical point when dropout begins to set in (Eyal & Woolard, 2013).

Figure 5.1 shows the extent of disparities in home resources for learners in different schooling environments. The graph represents a wide range of resources, and many interesting patterns emerge. There were general improvements in learner access to basic amenities such as running tap water and water-flush toilets. Between 2011 and 2015, access to water-flush toilets increased by 24 percentage points for learners in fee-paying schools and by only 13 percentage points for learners in no-fee schools. Eighty-four per cent of learners in independent

TIMSS 2015 Grade 9 National Report

schools had access to water-flush toilets in 2011 and this increased to 94 per cent in 2015. Similarly, over 90 per cent of learners in fee-paying and independent schools had access to running tap water in 2015, compared to only 64 per cent of learners in no-fee schools. This was an 11 percentage point improvement for learners in fee-paying schools compared to a five percentage point increase for no-fee school learners.

Figure 5.1: Percentage of learners with home resources in 2003, 2011 and 2015[a]

Resources at home	Public (2003)	No-fee (2011)	Fee-paying (2011)	Independent (2011)	No-fee (2015)	Fee-paying (2015)	Independent (2015)
Computer	33%	23%	44%	77%	22%	45%	72%
Own books		60%	68%	82%			
Internet connection		21%	38%	69%	45%	71%	84%
Own cell phone		74%	81%	92%	78%	86%	87%
Dictionary	78%	63%	81%	94%	71%	91%	96%
Electricity	80%	79%	92%	98%	88%	96%	98%
Running tap water	64%	59%	80%	92%	64%	91%	95%
Television	82%	82%	92%	98%	88%	97%	99%
Radio	92%	79%	85%	89%			
Water-flush toilets	48%	31%	66%	86%	44%	90%	94%
Motor car	38%	29%	47%	78%	42%	70%	86%
Telephone	54%	27%	34%	56%	12%	28%	46%
Fridge	73%	71%	86%	95%	89%	97%	99%

[a] In 2015, the question of whether learners had 'books of your very own' was not included.

It is encouraging that there were some resources where access was common. Nearly all learners in fee-paying and independent schools had access to electricity and electricity-dependent assets such as a fridge and a television. Nearly 90 per cent of learners in no-fee schools had similar access. In contrast, access to new technologies such as the internet and computers favoured learners in independent schools. Forty-five per cent of learners at no-fee schools reported having access to the internet at home in 2015, which was more than double the percentage reported in 2011, and is also considerably higher than estimates from household surveys. The 2016 Community Survey reported that 11 per cent of households countrywide had an internet connection in their dwelling (Stats SA, 2016). Learners could also gain access to the internet via their cell phones. There is a statistically significant association between having internet access and having a cell phone. Thirty-eight per cent of no-fee school learners, 63 per cent of fee-paying and 74 per cent of independent school learners responded "yes" to having both internet access and a cell phone.

Access to a computer at home remained the same in all schooling environments between 2011 and 2015. This could be explained by the widespread use of new devices such as tablets and the availability of computer facilities at school, a point to which we will return later. The 2016 Community Survey estimates household ownership of computers, laptops or desktops at 25 per cent, which is similar to the percentage reported by learners in no-fee schools (Stats SA, 2016).

6. Socioeconomic status (SES)

Numerous education studies have confirmed that the link between academic achievement and indicators of SES is strong and consistent in South Africa (Lee, Zuze & Ross, 2005; Taylor & Yu, 2009; Van der Berg, 2008; Visser, Juan & Feza, 2015). Depending on the context, SES is represented by a combination of factors including parental education levels, home resources, the availability of books in the home, academic aspirations and the structural features of the home. There are many ways in which this relationship operates. South African learners whose parents are better educated and more likely to be employed tend to have better educational outcomes (Branson et al., 2012; Case & Deaton, 1999). Families with greater socioeconomic resources can pass advantage to their

Understanding mathematics and science achievement amongst Grade 9 learners in South Africa **31**

Learners and the home environment

children by providing them with the material resources to support schooling (Roksa & Potter, 2011). In contrast, children from high poverty homes may have less assistance with schoolwork, especially at higher grade levels (Caro, McDonald & Willms, 2009).

Children who are surrounded by hardship can struggle to see that education can make any difference to their future. This is not to say that less educated parents cannot support their children's education. There are many ways in which parents of different backgrounds can remain engaged in their children's schooling careers and there is evidence to show that socioeconomically disadvantaged parents can do so effectively (Watt, 2016). However, high achievers from lower socioeconomic circumstances remain the exception rather than the norm owing to the many obstacles that these learners must overcome (Harris & Robinson, 2016).

6.1   Socioeconomic status (SES) asset quintiles

An asset-based index of SES was constructed by using principal components analysis. It was based on the method used by Taylor and Yu (2009) to investigate the significance of SES in educational achievement. The student SES variable was derived based on the availability of 16 assets in a learner's home[8]. Learners were grouped into one of five SES quintiles[9], with quintile 1 identifying the lowest SES and quintile 5 the highest. There was a clear split in SES levels between no-fee schools on the one hand and fee-paying and independent schools on the other. In no-fee schools, nearly three-quarters of learners were in the three lowest SES quintiles. In fee-paying and independent schools, the majority of learners were in the highest SES quintile; 43 per cent of learners in fee-paying schools and 64 per cent of learners in independent schools. Less than eight per cent of learners in fee-paying public and independent schools were in the lowest SES quintile compared to 30 per cent of learners in the no-fee system.

Figure 6.1: Percentage of learners by SES quintile and school type, 2015

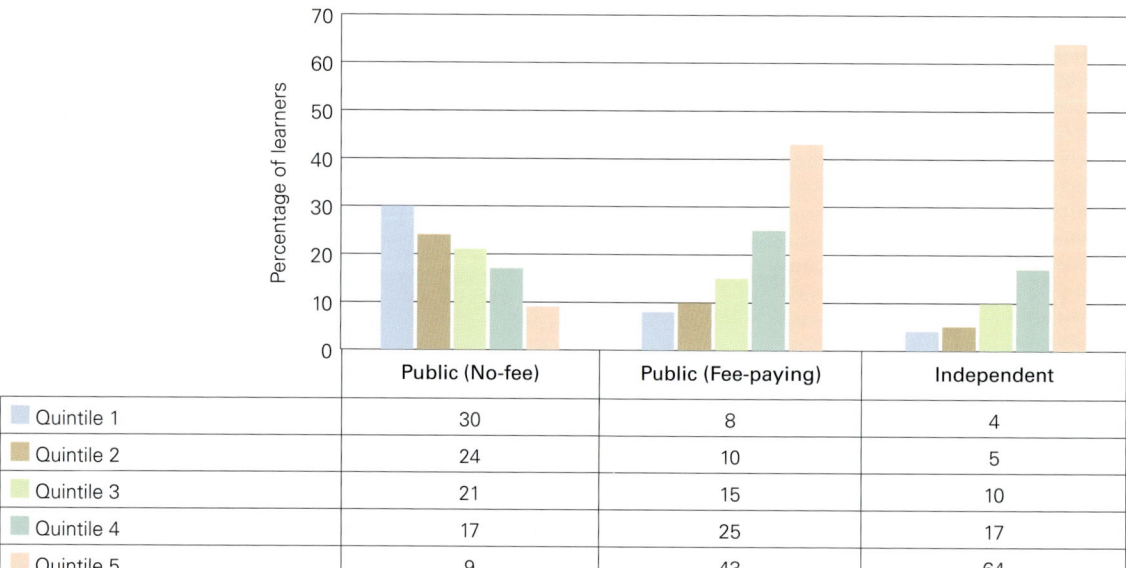

	Public (No-fee)	Public (Fee-paying)	Independent
Quintile 1	30	8	4
Quintile 2	24	10	5
Quintile 3	21	15	10
Quintile 4	17	25	17
Quintile 5	9	43	64

---

[8] *Assets included were as follows: a computer or tablet of your own, a computer or tablet that is shared with other people at home, study desk/table for your use, your own room, internet connection, your own cell phone, a gaming system, a dictionary, electricity, running tap water, television, DVD player, water-flush toilet, motor car, landline telephone, a fridge.*

[9] *The quintile used for SES was calculated by the TIMSS South Africa team. It is not the same as the poverty quintile that is assigned by the DBE.*

6.2 Parental education

Table 6.1 compares average achievement scores based on information provided by learners on their parents' education level. Between 2003 and 2015, average achievement increased at all parental education levels. Learners whose parents were better educated consistently achieved better test scores in mathematics and science. However, the gap has narrowed, especially for mathematics. In 2003, the mathematics achievement gap between learners whose parents had a post-schooling qualification and learners whose parents had completed at most primary school was 71 points. In 2015, the gap had reduced to 57 points.

Table 6.1: Average achievement by parental education levels, 2003, 2011 and 2015

	Average achievement score (SE)[a]			
	Primary schooling or lower	Secondary	Post-schooling	Do not know
Mathematics 2003	259 (5.5)	278 (4.0)	330 (8.9)	299 (8.7)
Mathematics 2011	318 (4.2)	344 (2.7)	389 (3.7)	366 (4.0)
Mathematics 2015	338 (3.8)	356 (3.2)	395 (6.5)	383 (5.6)
Science 2003	245 (6.9)	257 (5.3)	324 (10.3)	279 (10.4)
Science 2011	285 (5.9)	321 (3.9)	382 (4.9)	351 (5.3)
Science 2015	313 (4.9)	338 (4.0)	387 (8.0)	374 (6.8)

[a] Readers should note that five per cent of the responses to the question on parental education were missing.

Changes in parental education levels for learners attending different types of schools are compared in Figure 6.2 for 2011 and 2015. Parents of learners attending independent schools were the most highly educated but there was a noticeable increase in the percentage of parents with a post-schooling qualification in public schools. During this period, parents with a post-schooling qualification increased by nine percentage points in no-fee schools and by 11 percentage points in fee-paying schools. The levels of parental education reported by Grade 9 learners in TIMSS are higher than responses from the General Household Survey (DBE, 2016c). This difference could be because learners increasingly feel the need to exaggerate their parents' education level or simply because they do not know what the correct education level is and are guessing.

Figure 6.2: Changes in parental education levels by school type, 2011 and 2015

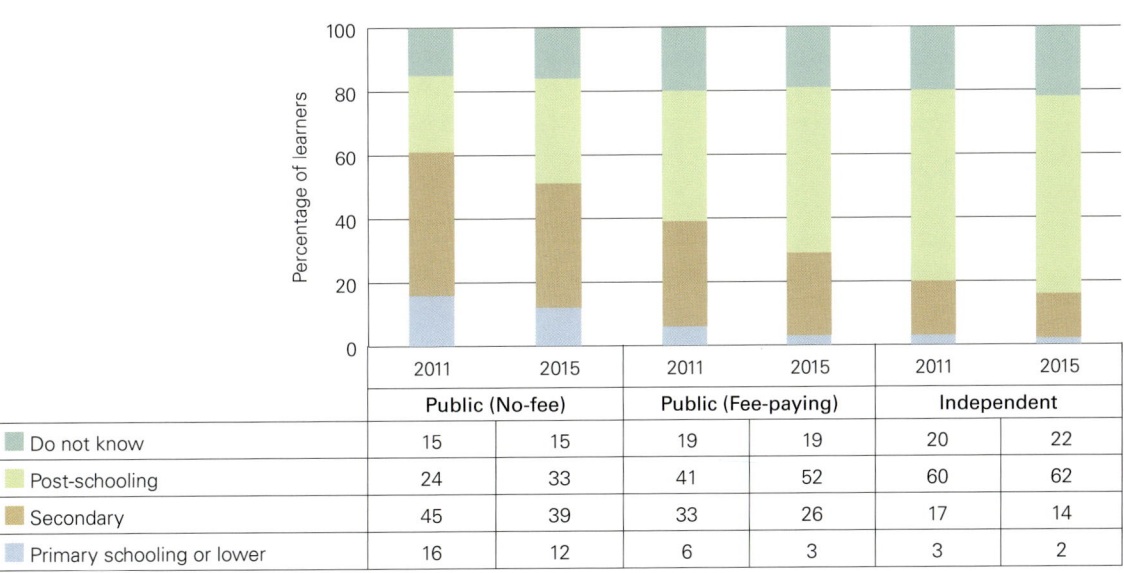

	Public (No-fee)		Public (Fee-paying)		Independent	
	2011	2015	2011	2015	2011	2015
Do not know	15	15	19	19	20	22
Post-schooling	24	33	41	52	60	62
Secondary	45	39	33	26	17	14
Primary schooling or lower	16	12	6	3	3	2

Learners and the home environment

6.3   Learner attitudes about mathematics and science

The positive association between attitudes and achievement is significant in many different countries, including top-performing Asian countries like Malaysia and Singapore (OECD, 2013b; Thien & Ong, 2015). Results from TIMSS 2011 found that learners who had positive attitudes about mathematics and science achieved better average test scores, even when other factors such as gender and SES were taken into account (Reddy, Juan, Zuze, Namome & Hannan, 2016c). TIMSS uses three indicators to identify learner attitudes about mathematics and science. The first is based on whether a learner finds the subjects enjoyable. The second is based on the value attached to mathematics and science in terms of their general usefulness to learners and to society. The third is the self-confidence in their ability to perform specific activities or tasks related to the subject areas (sometimes referred to as self-efficacy). The relationship between attitudes and achievement can move in both directions. Learners with more positive attitudes may approach the subject with greater ease and thus thrive. On the other hand, learners who do well may react by developing a better outlook about the subjects (Cates & Rhymer, 2003; Foley et al., 2017). Or, attitudes could be unrelated to performance and have more to do with the learning environment (Swars, Daane & Giesen, 2006).

Figure 6.3 summarises attitudes about mathematics and science among Grade 9 learners in 2011 and 2015. Learners attached a high value to mathematics. More than 70 per cent of learners attached a high value to mathematics in both 2011 and 2015. Only 39 per cent of learners were in the highest category for enjoyment of mathematics, with little change over time. In spite of valuing and enjoying mathematics, confidence in the subject was extremely low. Only 10 per cent were highly confident in mathematics and the percentage with low confidence increased between 2011 and 2015.

Compared to mathematics, the percentage of learners who attached a high value to science was lower but enjoyment of science was higher when compared to mathematics. Again, only 10 per cent of learners expressed a high confidence in their science abilities, with a seven percentage point decline from 2011.

Figure 6.3: Changes in enjoyment of, value attached to and confidence in mathematics and science, 2011 and 2015

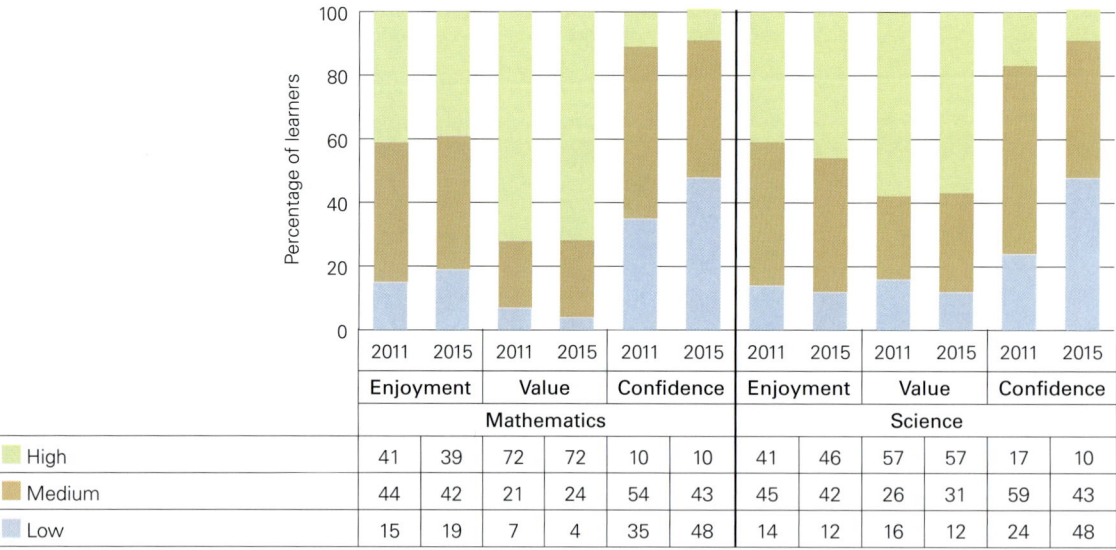

		2011	2015	2011	2015	2011	2015	2011	2015	2011	2015	2011	2015
		Enjoyment		Value		Confidence		Enjoyment		Value		Confidence	
		Mathematics						Science					
■	High	41	39	72	72	10	10	41	46	57	57	17	10
■	Medium	44	42	21	24	54	43	45	42	26	31	59	43
■	Low	15	19	7	4	35	48	14	12	16	12	24	48

In Table 6.2, the relationship between attitudes and achievement is compared across schooling environments. The relationship between attitude levels and achievement was positive in both subject areas. Learners who were highly positive about mathematics and science achieved higher average test scores than those with a less positive outlook, who achieved the lower average scores.

Table 6.2: Average achievement by learner attitudes towards mathematics and science and school type, 2015

	High (SE)	Medium (SE)	Low (SE)
Enjoyment (mathematics)			
Public (No-fee)	363 (3.4)	328 (3.8)	324 (4.6)
Public (Fee-paying)	438 (11.9)	415 (11.4)	421 (8.8)
Independent	488 (13.9)	485 (15)	457 (8.7)
Enjoyment (science)			
Public (No-fee)	348 (4.3)	297 (4.2)	279 (6.4)
Public (Fee-paying)	440 (13.3)	416 (12.8)	414 (11.9)
Independent	497 (14.6)	471 (10.8)	486 (24.9)
Valuing (mathematics)			
Public (No-fee)	353 (3.3)	322 (4.1)	292 (5.6)
Public (Fee-paying)	427 (10.5)	421 (10.3)	400 (13.8)
Independent	479 (12.4)	480 (14.2)	455 (21.5)
Valuing (science)			
Public (No-fee)	332 (4.1)	300 (5.1)	306 (7.2)
Public (Fee-paying)	428 (14.5)	413 (12.1)	443 (8.7)
Independent	492 (13.9)	479 (13.4)	484 (12.5)
Confidence (mathematics)			
Public (No-fee)	402 (4.8)	346 (3.7)	328 (3.3)
Public (Fee-paying)	490 (12.3)	431 (10.9)	404 (9.4)
Independent	556 (23.4)	485 (10.8)	439 (9.0)
Confidence (science)			
Public (No-fee)	370 (5.7)	316 (4.1)	293 (4.2)
Public (Fee-paying)	461 (13.6)	425 (12.7)	411 (12.2)
Independent	518 (20.4)	477 (10.1)	471 (15.6)

6.4 Learner academic aspirations

Learners begin to think about their lives beyond school from an early age, which may influence how they approach their schoolwork. TIMSS 2011 identified important differences in how far learners intended to progress in their studies. Learners in no-fee schools, and boys in particular, had the lowest aspirations for traditional tertiary studies (Zuze et al., 2015).

In 2015, learners were asked how far they expected to go in their academic careers and the results are compared in Figure 6.4 on page 36. Broadly speaking, the academic ambitions of learners in fee-paying schools and independent schools followed a similar pattern. Most learners set their sights on a post-secondary school qualification. The academic ambitions of learners in no-fee schools seem to lie at the extremes. On the one hand were learners with very low academic aspirations. It is estimated that 12 per cent of young South Africans do not complete Grade 9 each year, leaving them with limited opportunities (DBE, 2016c). Five per cent of learners in no-fee schools viewed their academic careers as ending at Grade 9 and 16 per cent were only aspiring to complete Grade 12. On the other hand were the 34 per cent of learners in no-fee schools who aimed to complete a doctoral degree. Aspirations for further studies were higher in fee-paying and independent schools. Seventy-one per cent of learners in fee-paying schools and 83 per cent of learners in independent schools aspired to completing an honours degree or further. Also worth noting was the 37 per cent of learners in fee-paying schools and 42 per cent in independent schools who were aiming for a doctoral degree.

PART B

Learners and the home environment

Figure 6.4: Learners' educational aspirations by school type, 2015

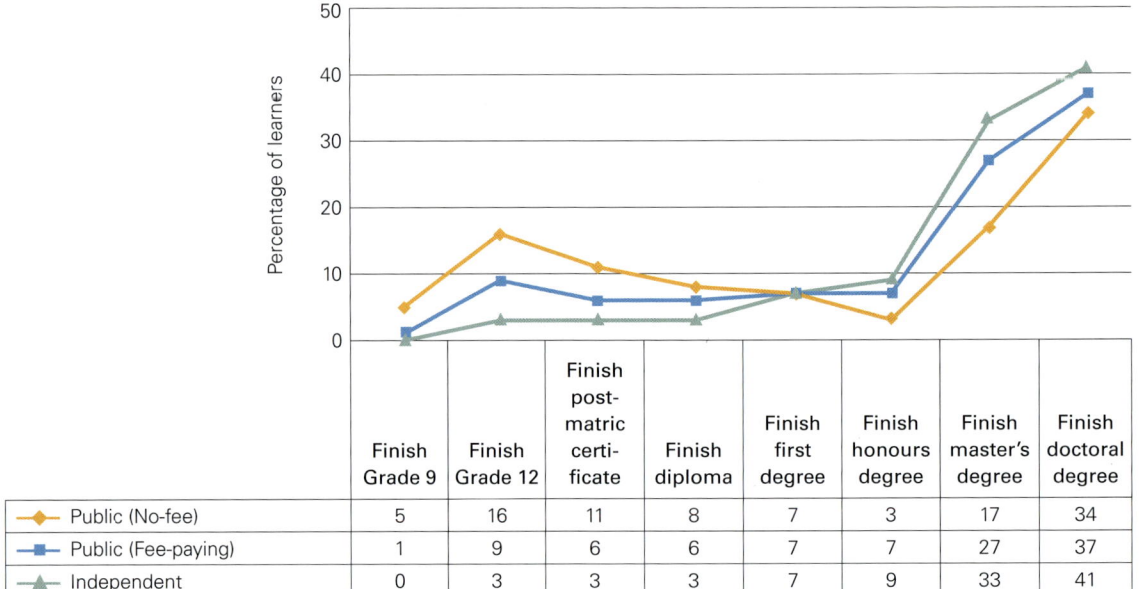

	Finish Grade 9	Finish Grade 12	Finish post-matric certi-ficate	Finish diploma	Finish first degree	Finish honours degree	Finish master's degree	Finish doctoral degree
Public (No-fee)	5	16	11	8	7	3	17	34
Public (Fee-paying)	1	9	6	6	7	7	27	37
Independent	0	3	3	3	7	9	33	41

Section summary

Many South African learners live in impoverished communities. Disparities in access to home resources underscore the persistence of poverty and inequality in the country. The gap in home resources between learners in the no-fee and fee-paying components of the education system remains wide. This raises the stakes for the role that the school system needs to play in order for education to be an equaliser. Parents of learners who attended independent schools were more highly educated but the levels of education among parents of learners in public schools have increased substantially. Information provided by learners about parental education levels needs to be read with caution because they are considerably higher than reports from household surveys. Learner attitudes about mathematics and science were very subject specific. Learners attached a higher value to mathematics than to science but confidence levels were low in both subjects. Attitudes were positively associated with average mathematics and science achievement. Educational aspirations were higher for learners in better-resourced schools but a pool of learners in each school grouping harboured ambitions for obtaining advanced degrees. Parental support for learning goes beyond the resources that parents can provide. The many ways that learners can be supported outside of school will be the focus of the next section.

PART C

SUPPORT FOR LEARNING OUTSIDE OF SCHOOL

Support for learning outside of school

The private resources for education continue to separate learners in South Africa, but there are other mechanisms for parents to support schooling that are less reliant on income levels. Families should be able to support the academic and emotional development of their children in different ways (Sebastian, Moon & Cunningham, 2017; Wilder, 2014). Parents and caregivers can ensure that what is learned at school is reinforced with homework and other activities. They can engage with teachers and encourage their children to have a positive outlook about learning (Hoover-Dempsey et al., 2001; Wang & Sheikh-Khalil, 2014). They can also make sure that their children have sufficient time to complete homework. Many of these activities are inter-related and so they tend to reinforce each other. The reality is that the lives of learners in high-poverty communities can be full of disruptions. Aside from the external home environment, children themselves have different perspectives about mathematics and science, which means that some will approach subjects like mathematics and science with greater ease than others.

7. Homework and homework checking

Grade 9 learners were asked how often their teachers gave them mathematics and science homework. Nationally, 68 per cent of learners reported receiving mathematics homework every day and only three per cent stated that they received homework less than once a week. Learners in public schools received homework more regularly than learners in independent schools. However, it is not clear whether learners in independent schools were assigned more lengthy homework less frequently or whether work was, in fact, completed during class time.

Figure 7.1: Frequency of receiving mathematics homework by school type, 2015

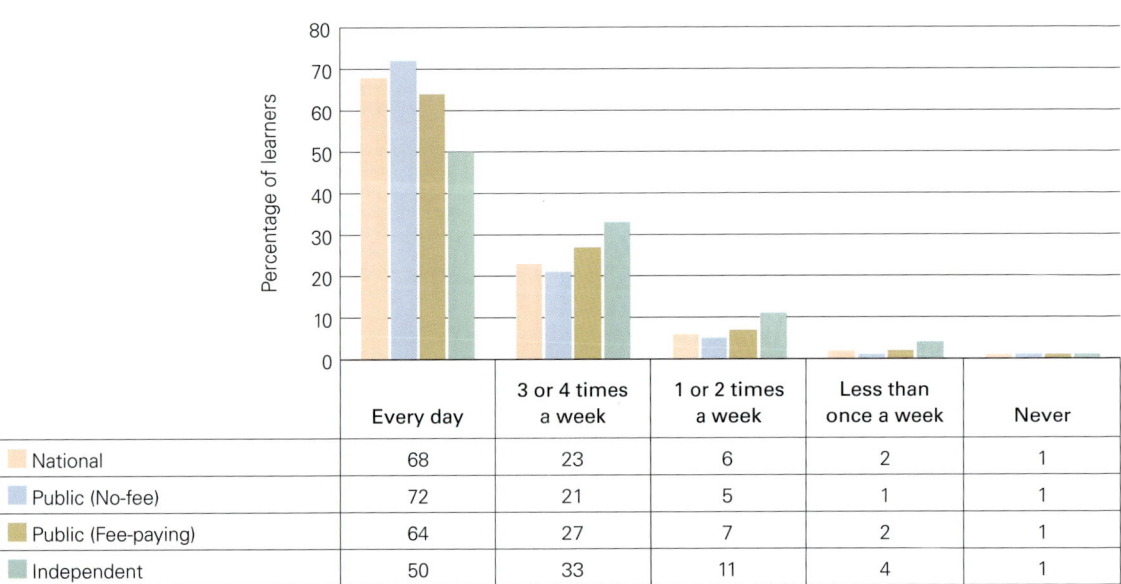

	Every day	3 or 4 times a week	1 or 2 times a week	Less than once a week	Never
National	68	23	6	2	1
Public (No-fee)	72	21	5	1	1
Public (Fee-paying)	64	27	7	2	1
Independent	50	33	11	4	1

Learners in public schools received homework more regularly than learners in independent schools. However, it is not clear whether learners in independent schools were assigned more lengthy homework less frequently or whether work was, in fact, completed during class time.

Learners received science homework less frequently. Less than a quarter of learners received science homework daily and 11 per cent of learners received science homework less than once a week. Learners in no-fee schools received science homework more often than learners in fee-paying or independent schools but once again, the length or complexity of the homework assignments could not be determined.

Figure 7.2: Frequency of receiving science homework by school type, 2015

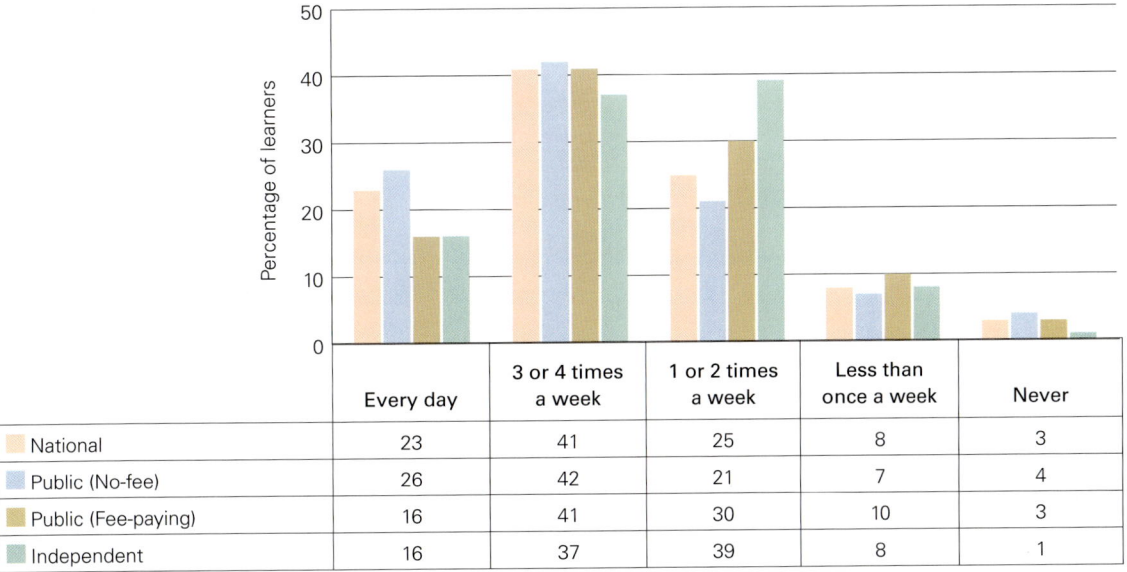

	Every day	3 or 4 times a week	1 or 2 times a week	Less than once a week	Never
National	23	41	25	8	3
Public (No-fee)	26	42	21	7	4
Public (Fee-paying)	16	41	30	10	3
Independent	16	37	39	8	1

One way that parents can remain engaged with learner progress is by checking homework. The mere act of checking homework is useful and important but if parents understand the content, it is easier for them to assist learners more directly. This is not always the case as can be seen in Figure 7.3. Only 30 per cent of learners in no-fee schools reported that it was either 'never' or 'almost never' a problem for their parents to understand the language used in schoolwork. Difficulties in comprehension were less of a problem among parents in fee-paying and independent schools. Sixty-one per cent of learners in fee-paying schools and 69 per cent of learners in independent schools reported that the language of schoolwork was 'never' or 'almost never' a problem.

Support for learning outside of school

Figure 7.3: Schoolwork is in a language that parents/caregivers don't understand by school type, 2015

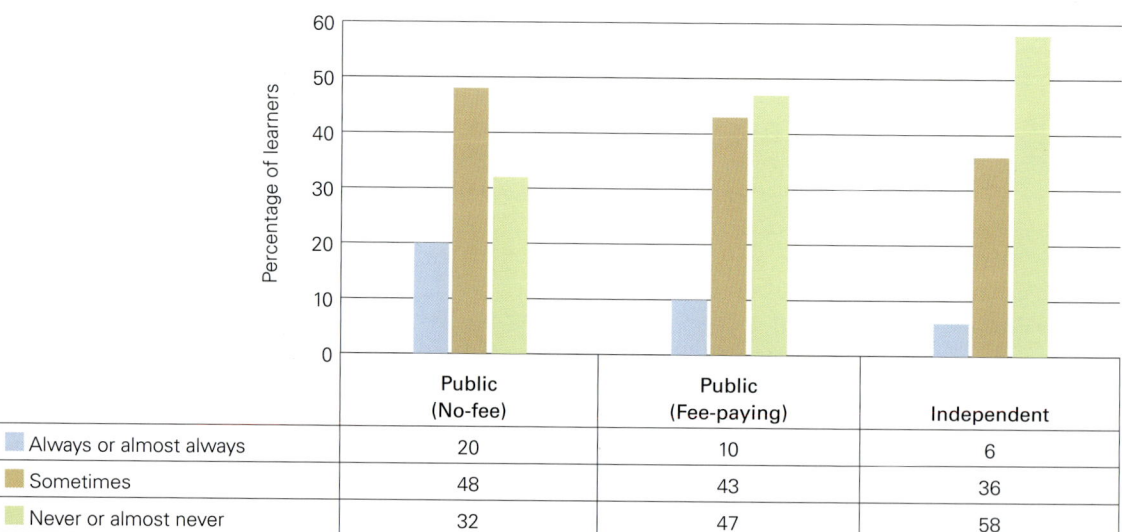

	Public (No-fee)	Public (Fee-paying)	Independent
Always or almost always	21	11	6
Sometimes	49	28	25
Never or almost never	30	61	69

In Figure 7.4 the question of whether the level of difficulty of schoolwork prevents parents from assisting learners is explored. As before, the challenges faced by parents of learners in no-fee schools were greater. For one in five learners in no-fee schools, the level of difficulty of schoolwork was too high for their parents to be able to assist them. These learners stated that schoolwork was 'always or almost always' so difficult that parents or caregivers were unable to provide support. Only one in ten learners in fee-paying schools and one in twenty learners in independent schools were in the same position.

Figure 7.4: Schoolwork is so difficult that parents/caregivers are not able to help by school type, 2015

	Public (No-fee)	Public (Fee-paying)	Independent
Always or almost always	20	10	6
Sometimes	48	43	36
Never or almost never	32	47	58

The correlation between the frequency of checking homework and achievement is not straightforward. Table 7.1 shows that average achievement in both mathematics and science was higher for learners whose schoolwork was checked less frequently. This would suggest that learners who are finding the content difficult have their homework checked more frequently and parents tend to review the work of academically stronger learners less often. However, the previous graph clearly shows that some parents struggle to understand the homework content. The act of checking homework is therefore no guarantee of support if parents cannot provide constructive input.

Table 7.1: Average achievement by frequency of checking homework by school type, 2015

	Mathematics (SE)			Science (SE)		
	Public (No-fee)	Public (Fee-paying)	Independent	Public (No-fee)	Public (Fee-paying)	Independent
Every day or almost every day	341 (3.0)	406 (9.1)	446 (9.4)	317 (3.9)	405 (11.3)	447 (11.1)
Once or twice a week	348 (4.1)	428 (9.7)	474 (11.3)	326 (5.1)	432 (11.8)	487 (14.6)
Once or twice a month	352 (6.1)	443 (13.7)	495 (20.0)	331 (8.4)	446 (15.8)	500 (19.5)
Never or almost never	346 (5.1)	454 (12.0)	507 (19.6)	323 (6.7)	461 (13.9)	521 (17.7)

8.   Extra lessons

The demand for extra lessons in mathematics and science is high in South Africa. Extra lessons are provided through private tuition and through franchised organisations. Learners attend lessons either individually or in groups. The TIMSS 2015 study asked learners who took extra mathematics and science lessons why they needed to do so[10]. Figure 8.1 summarises the reasons that learners gave for taking extra mathematics and science lessons. Average achievement and SEs are also shown on the graph. A higher percentage of learners in no-fee schools attended extra lessons to excel in class and also to keep up in class. Forty-four per cent of learners in no-fee schools took extra mathematics lessons to excel in class. Only 36 per cent of learners in fee-paying schools and independent schools gave the same reason. Average achievement in mathematics was highest in each school type for learners who took extra lessons to excel in class when compared to learners who took part to keep up in class. The motivation for taking extra lessons in science was reversed. A higher percentage of learners took extra science lessons to keep up in class than to excel in class. Average science test scores were similar irrespective of the reason for taking extra science lessons. Again, a higher percentage of learners in no-fee schools were enrolled in extra science lessons.

Average achievement in mathematics was highest in each school type for learners who took extra lessons to excel in class when compared to learners who took part to keep up in class. The motivation for taking extra lessons in science was reversed.

---

[10] The TIMSS questionnaire made it clear that questions about extra lessons did not refer to lessons provided by the school.

Support for learning outside of school

Figure 8.1: Percentage of learners by reason for extra lessons and school type, 2015

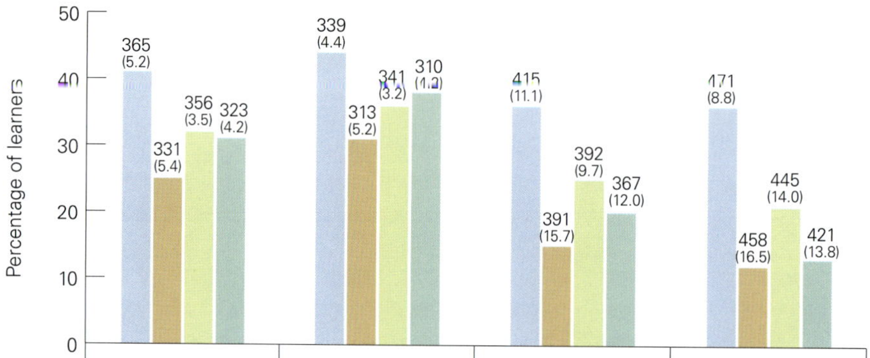

	National	Public (No-fee)	Public (Fee-paying)	Independent
Yes, to excel in maths class	41	44	36	36
Yes, to excel in science class	25	31	15	12
Yes, to keep up in maths class	32	36	25	21
Yes, to keep up in science class	31	38	20	13

Section summary

Although learners attending public schools received mathematics and science homework more frequently, the length or complexity of the homework assignments could not be established. Learners attending no-fee schools reported that their parents struggled with the language and complexity of schoolwork more frequently. A higher percentage of learners in public schools were involved in extra lessons. Because these questions referred to extra lessons that were arranged outside of school, it raises questions about who was responsible for organising them. The reason for taking part in extra lessons depended on the subject matter. For mathematics, the main motivation was to excel in class and for science it was to keep up with the subject matter. Learners with lower average test scores attended extra lessons in greater numbers.

PART **D**

A COMPARISON OF THE SCHOOLING ENVIRONMENT

A comparison of the schooling environment

Learners from public schools seek support for their studies through external support programmes in far greater numbers than learners in other schooling environments.

Previous sections of this report showed that learners from public schools, particularly no-fee schools, come from homes that have fewer physical resources at home, and have less-educated parents who are also more likely to struggle to understand the content of a learner's schoolwork. Learners from public schools seek support for their studies through external support programmes in far greater numbers than learners in other schooling environments. The multiple disadvantages faced by learners from poor homes make the role of schools all the more important. The following section focuses on access to key physical resources across schooling environments. We considered specific school resources that have been the focal point of recent DBE policy (textbooks, libraries, laboratories and computer resources) and that have a known positive relationship with achievement. We also discuss the results related to the climate[11] of the school as well as important aspects of the teaching and learning environment.

9.   School resources

9.1.   Textbook provision

There is general agreement that textbooks are an important resource to support teaching and learning, especially when used effectively. Textbook availability has improved. It has been found to have a significant relationship to academic achievement in many education systems, including South Africa (SACMEQ, 2010; Zuze & Reddy, 2014). The Draft National Policy for the Provision and Management of Learning and Teaching Support Material (LTSM) provides guidelines for the production and distribution of quality textbooks and workbooks (DBE, 2014). Textbooks, workbooks and teacher guides are core LTSMs because they are considered essential for covering the curriculum.

The provision of textbooks in South African public schools has been the focus of attention not only because of efforts by public interest organisations[12] but also because government made ambitious promises about book provisioning – for example the national workbooks programme. Figure 9.1 summarises learner responses to a question about whether or not they have their own mathematics and science textbooks. Nationally, 82 per cent of Grade 9 learners had access to their own mathematics textbook and 69 per cent had access to their own science textbook. However textbook availability was lower in no-fee schools. Seventy-eight per cent of learners in no-fee schools had their own mathematics text book in 2015, compared with 88 per cent in fee-paying schools and 85 per cent in independent schools. The gap in science textbook ownership between public and independent schools was wider than for mathematics. Sixty-six per cent of Grade 9 learners in no-fee schools had their own science textbook compared to 74 and 82 per cent in fee-paying and independent schools, respectively.

---

[11] The terms 'school culture', 'school climate' and 'school environment' are often used interchangeably but the general meaning of these terms are learners', parents' and school personnel's experience of school life and its associated norms, goals, values, interpersonal relationships, teaching and learning practices, and organisational structures (Rodwell, 2015).

[12] A Supreme Court ruling in 2012 guaranteed learners in public schools the right to prescribed textbooks at the beginning of the academic year. Some would argue that turning the spotlight on textbook delivery has been instrumental to raising national awareness on the issue (Veriava, 2013). Others maintain that the textbook crisis is a reflection of decades of corruption and financial mismanagement that need to be addressed for any lasting improvements to take root (Chisholm, 2013).

Figure 9.1: Percentage of learners who own a textbook by school type, 2015

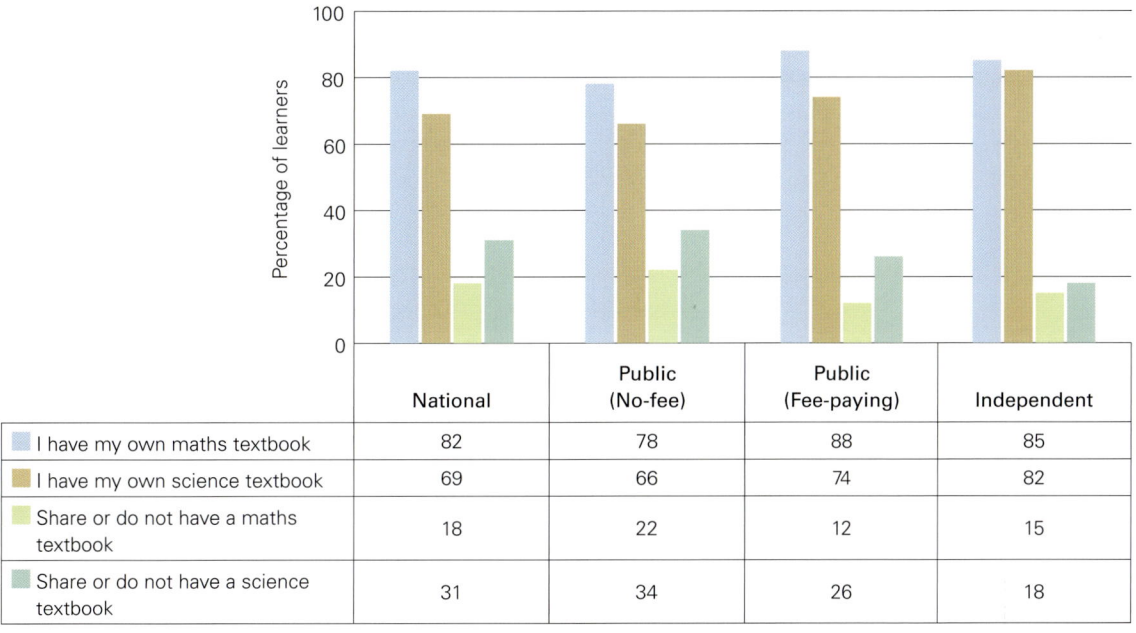

	National	Public (No-fee)	Public (Fee-paying)	Independent
▉ I have my own maths textbook	82	78	88	85
▉ I have my own science textbook	69	66	74	82
▉ Share or do not have a maths textbook	18	22	12	15
▉ Share or do not have a science textbook	31	34	26	18

How textbook ownership relates to mathematics and science achievement is dependent on the type of school. In no-fee schools, there was a clear positive relationship between textbook ownership and average test scores. In fee-paying and independent schools, learners who owned a textbook had an achievement advantage over others, but those who shared a textbook did not outperform those without any textbook. Learners without standard textbooks in better-resourced schools might have benefited from other learning resources (such as computer-based learning resources) that are not captured by this question.

Table 9.1: Average achievement by textbook ownership and school type, 2015

	Public (No-fee) (SE)	Public (Fee-paying) (SE)	Independent (SE)
Mathematics			
I have my own maths textbook	348 (3.5)	433 (10.0)	489 (13.0)
I share a maths textbook	328 (5.0)	360 (9.9)	406 (14.6)
I don't have a maths textbook	330 (10.5)	387 (10.5)	424 (18.9)
Science			
I have my own science textbook	329 (4.4)	448 (11.3)	502 (12.5)
I share a science textbook	305 (5.6)	350 (14.4)	391 (13.9)
I don't have a science textbook	302 (9.4)	403 (24.4)	429 (16.7)

A comparison of the schooling environment

In Figures 9.2 and 9.3, textbook ownership is considered at the provincial level. Responses were grouped into learners who had their own textbook and those who shared or did not have any textbook. Learners who reported that they owned their own mathematics textbook ranged from 90 per cent to 72 per cent. Availability was highest in the Western Cape, Gauteng and Limpopo and lowest in the Eastern Cape and KwaZulu-Natal.

Figure 9.2: Percentage of learners who own a mathematic textbook by province, 2015

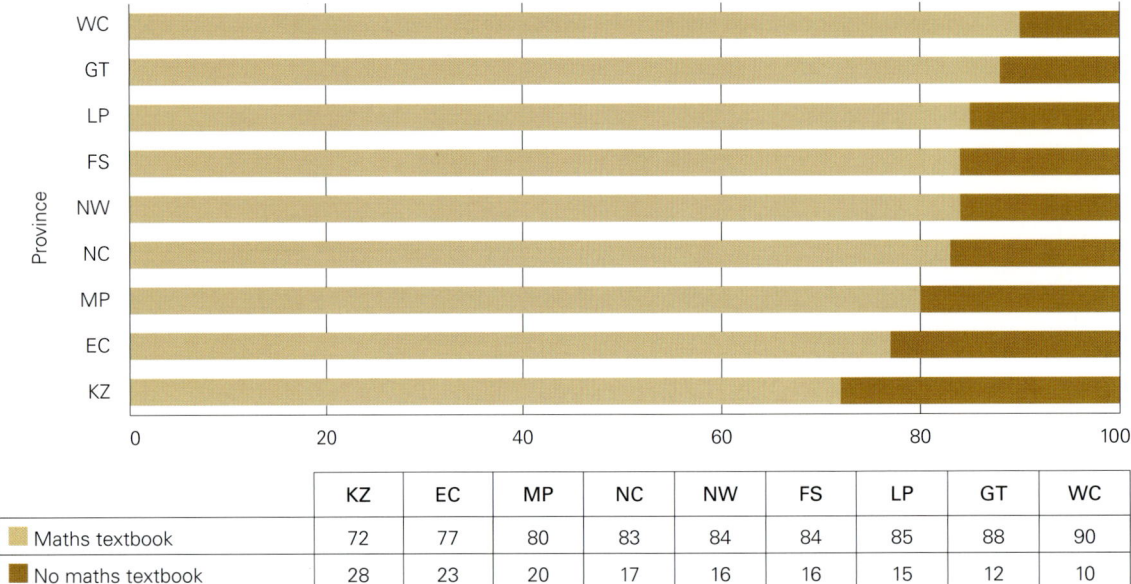

	KZ	EC	MP	NC	NW	FS	LP	GT	WC
Maths textbook	72	77	80	83	84	84	85	88	90
No maths textbook	28	23	20	17	16	16	15	12	10

Provincial differences in textbook ownership were greater for science. Availability ranged from 87 per cent in the Western Cape to 43 per cent in KwaZulu-Natal. Learners in the Free State, Gauteng and Limpopo had similar access to individual science textbooks. As with mathematics, learners in the Eastern Cape and KwaZulu-Natal had the most limited access.

Figure 9.3: Percentage of learners who own a science textbook by province, 2015

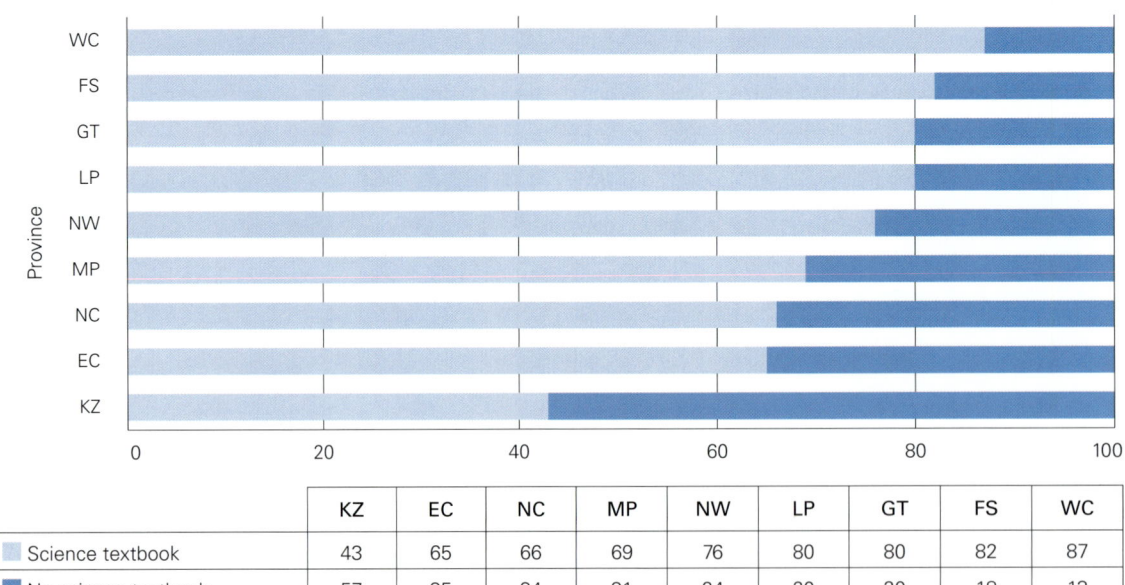

	KZ	EC	NC	MP	NW	LP	GT	FS	WC
Science textbook	43	65	66	69	76	80	80	82	87
No science textbook	57	35	34	31	24	20	20	18	13

In Table 9.2, trends in the use of mathematics textbooks and workbooks are explored. The percentage of learners whose teachers used mathematics textbooks as a basis of instruction increased from 34 per cent in 2003 to 73 per cent in 2015. Most of the increase occurred between 2003 and 2011. Along the same lines, the percentage of learners who received instruction from teachers who used science textbooks as a basis of instruction increased from 36 per cent in 2003 to 64 per cent in 2015. Again, most of the gains were made between 2003 and 2011, with a slight decline between 2011 and 2015. Just over half of learners were taught by teachers who used workbooks as a supplementary tool, with trends remaining constant between 2011 and 2015. These findings could reflect the effect of the draft policy on LTSM of 2014 which states that each learner and educator should be in possession of a core set of LTSMs, which should comprise a textbook or learner book, workbook and teacher guide.

Table 9.2: Percentage of learners whose teachers use each resource type, 2003, 2011 and 2015

	Textbooks (SE)		Workbooks or worksheets (SE)	
	Basis for instruction	Supplementary	Basis for instruction	Supplementary
Mathematics				
Mathematics 2003	34 (4.0)	60 (3.9)	–	–
Mathematics 2011	71 (3.5)	27 (3.4)	43 (3.7)	51 (3.7)
Mathematics 2015	73 (3.1)	27 (3.1)	47 (3.9)	52 (3.9)
Science				
Science 2003	36 (3.3)	56 (3.5)	–	–
Science 2011	66 (3.6)	28 (3.2)	39 (3.8)	52 (3.7)
Science 2015	64 (3.7)	32 (3.5)	37 (2.8)	54 (3.0)

9.2   Computer resources

The effective use of computer technology in schools has been part of government's long-term strategy for over a decade (DoE, 2004). Among the goals listed in the DBE's Action Plan to 2019 are improving the computer literacy of teachers and increasing access to computers among South African learners (DBE, 2016d).

Principals were asked to indicate how many computers (including tablets) for use by Grade 9 learners were available at the school. Since the TIMSS sample is only representative on the learner level, responses of principals and teachers are given in relation to the number of learners involved. Figure 9.4 shows that access to computer facilities at school is still heavily skewed towards better-resourced schools. Seventy per cent of Grade 9 learners in no-fee schools did not have computers that they could use at school in 2015. Although better, 51 per cent of learners in fee-paying schools were in the same position. Only 23 per cent of learners in independent schools were without access to computers. Furthermore, where there was access, the number of computers was higher in independent schools. To be interpreted more clearly, it would be important to understand how computers are integrated into teaching activities, but access does appear to be extremely uneven across South African schools.

> Among the goals listed in the DBE's Action Plan to 2019 are improving the computer literacy of teachers and increasing access to computers among South African learners (DBE, 2016d).

A comparison of the schooling environment

Figure 9.4: Percentage of learners with access to school computer facilities by school type, 2015

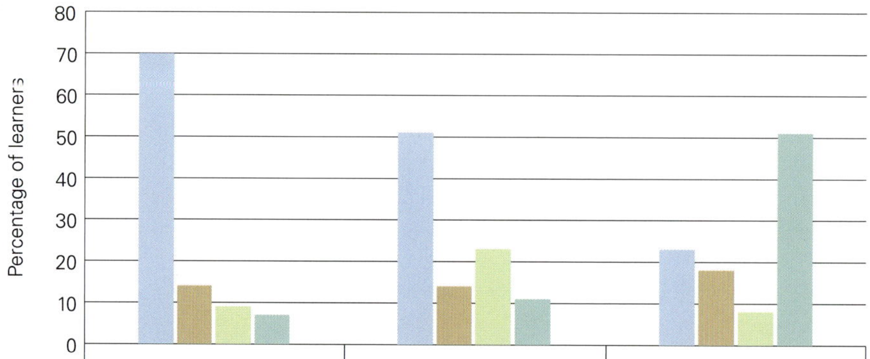

	Public (No-fee)	Public (Fee-paying)	Independent
No computers at school	70	51	23
1 – 24 computers	14	14	18
25 – 49 computers	9	23	8
50 and more computers	7	11	51

9.3   Library and laboratory facilities

The National Guidelines for School Library and Information Services describe a number of options for the provision of library resources at schools. These include: a centralised school library, mobile libraries, classroom libraries, cluster libraries and school community libraries (DBE, 2012b).

Earlier in this section, we described how learners in public schools were less able to access individual mathematics and science textbooks. Figure 9.5 reflects the provision of library facilities across South African schools based on TIMSS 2015. The availability of library facilities was most limited for learners in no-fee schools. Only 33 per cent of learners in no-fee schools had a library at school. Learners attending fee-paying schools were more likely to attend a school with a library than learners attending independent schools. Sixty-four per cent of learners at fee-paying schools had access to a school library compared to 52 per cent of their peers in independent schools. Many independent schools have started to integrate ICT into teaching and learning. At these schools, learners would tend to access online resources as opposed to physical libraries.

Figure 9.5: Percentage of learners with access to school library facilities by school type, 2015

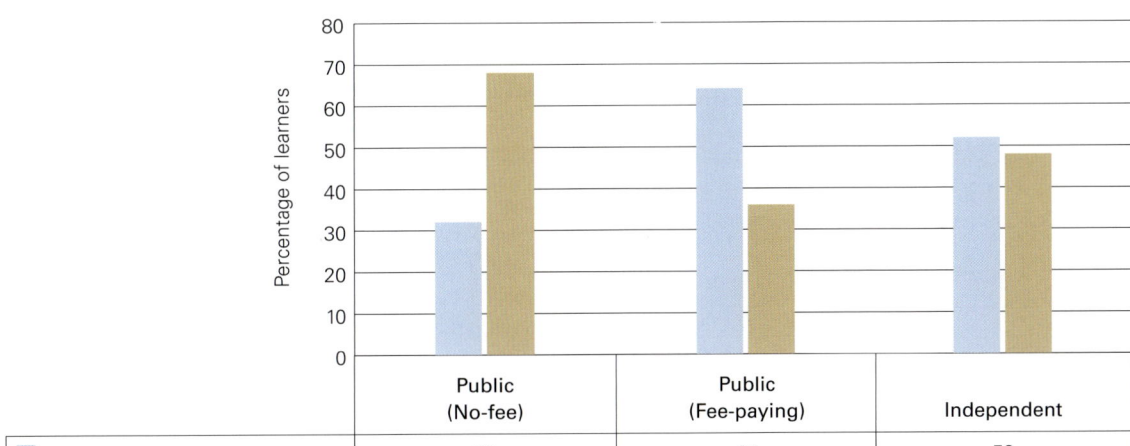

	Public (No-fee)	Public (Fee-paying)	Independent
Yes	32	64	52
No	68	36	48

Access to science laboratories followed a similar pattern to access to school libraries. Only 34 per cent of learners in no-fee schools could access a science laboratory. Access was higher in fee-paying schools than in independent schools according to the TIMSS 2015 results shown in Figure 9.6.

Figure 9.6: Percentage of learners with access to science laboratory by school type, 2015

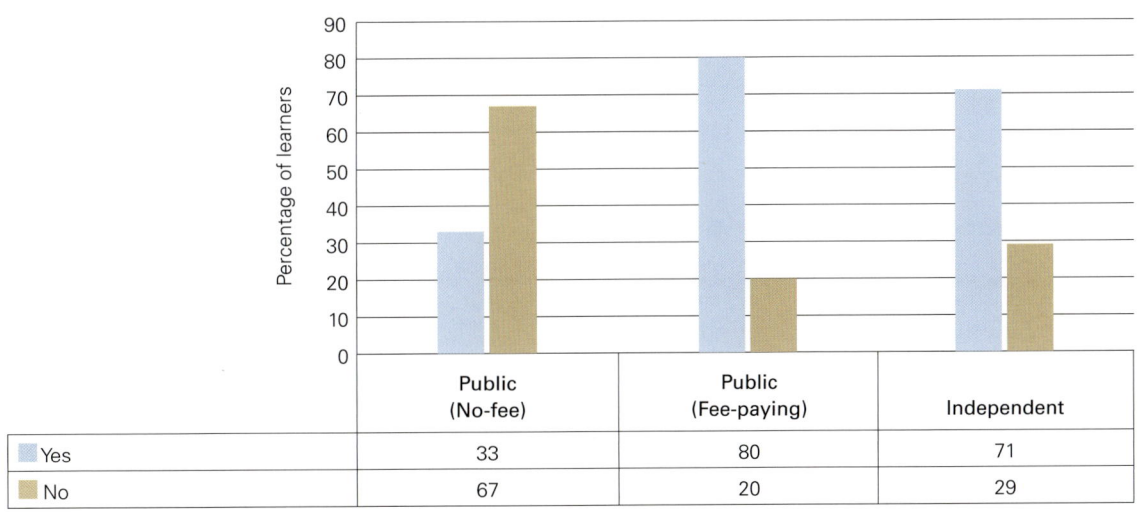

	Public (No-fee)	Public (Fee-paying)	Independent
Yes	33	80	71
No	67	20	29

A comparison of the schooling environment

9.4   School meals

The DBE runs a NSNP with the aim of providing nutritious meals to learners in the poorest schools across the country. Primary and secondary schools classified in the DBE in quintiles 1 to 3 (i.e. no-fee schools) qualify for this assistance and learners should be provided with a meal on every school day. Between 2013 and 2014, the programme reached an average of 9.2 million learners in 19 383 quintile 1 to 3 primary, secondary and special schools (DBE, 2015b). Virtually all no-fee schools benefited from the school nutrition programme as shown in Figure 9.7. While school meals were also provided in other school groupings, these were likely to be funded through school fees or other private means.

Figure 9.7: Availability of school meals by school type, 2015

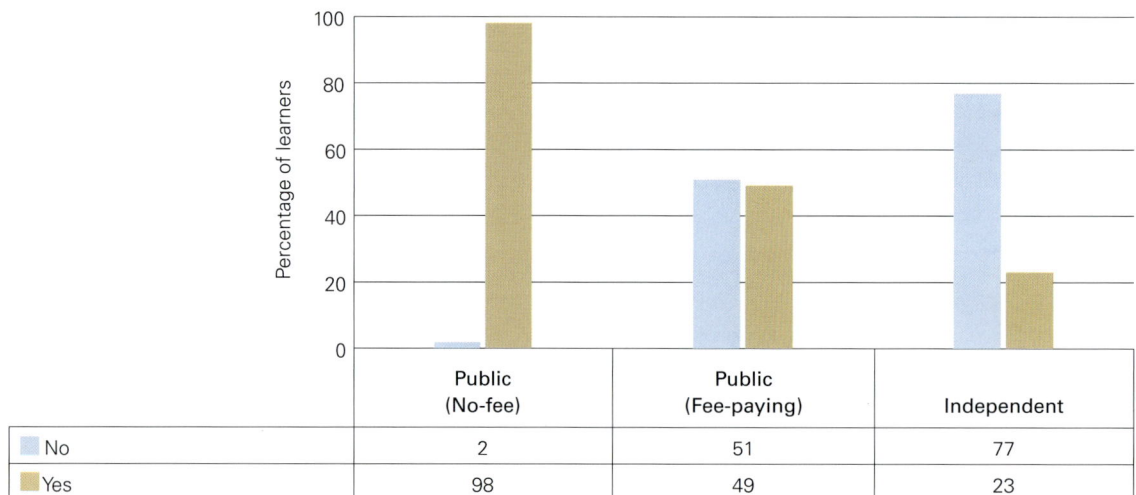

	Public (No-fee)	Public (Fee-paying)	Independent
No	2	51	77
Yes	98	49	23

10.   School climate

The climate of the school consists of many aspects of the educational environment. It includes the values and outlook of the school; the relationships among learners, teachers, parents and school administrators; the organisational structure and the teaching and learning practices (Thapa, Cohen, Higgins-D'Alessandro & Guffey, 2012). School climate is not just about school safety, although this is the impression sometimes given; perhaps because of media attention focusing on episodes of violence. Legislation exists to protect children from the worst forms of physical violence, such as corporal punishment (Burton & Leoschut, 2013). However, these requirements are not always enforced. Analysis of TIMSS 2011 data showed that a school's climate was associated with better TIMSS test scores (Zuze et al., 2016). In this section we focus on a range of school climate indicators, including school academic expectations, the organisational structure as well as levels of school violence.

10.1   An overview of school climate across South African schools

Figure 10.1 provides an overview of school climate in South African schools based on some of the indicators that will be described below, as well as others that were collected but are not discussed at length here. There are striking differences in the climate of different schooling environments but there are some important exceptions. Learners in public schools faced less orderly environments, greater disciplinary problems and more widespread bullying than learners in independent schools. The situation was worse in no-fee schools. Learners in independent schools were taught by teachers with higher job satisfaction. None of the learners in independent schools were taught by teachers who reported facing many challenges to their work. Challenges teachers faced included in the index presented here were: having too large class sizes, too much material to cover in class, too many teaching hours, too many administrative tasks, too much pressure from parents, the need for more time to prepare for class and to assist individual learners, and having difficulty in keeping up with curriculum changes. Less than half of learners in public schools were taught by teachers who were very satisfied with their job. The percentage of learners in independent schools where academic success was emphasised was three times as high as the percentage reported in no-fee schools. However, a higher sense of school belonging was reported in no-fee schools in comparison to fee-paying or independent schools.

Figure 10.1: A summary of school climate in South African schools by school type, 2015

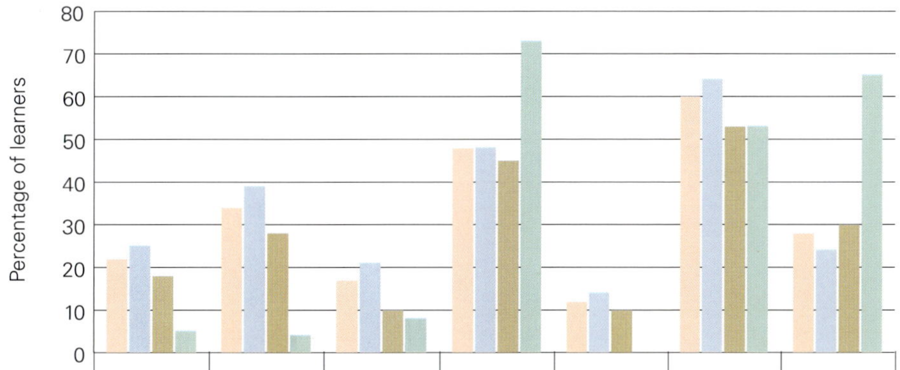

	Less than safe and orderly	Severe problems with discipline and safety	Learners being bullied on a weekly basis	Teachers very satisfied with their job	Many challenges facing teachers	Higher sense of school belonging	High emphasis on academic success
National	22	34	17	48	12	60	28
Public (No-fee)	25	39	21	48	14	64	24
Public (Fee-paying)	18	28	10	45	10	53	30
Independent	5	4	8	73	0	53	65

10.2 Emphasis placed on academic success

School principals were asked to respond to 13 statements that characterised the emphasis that the school placed on academic success. Statements included the attitudes of teachers, parents and learners at the school with reference to teachers' understanding of the curriculum, parental and teacher expectations, parental involvement, learners' commitment to academic standards and learners' respect for peers who excel in school. Responses to these statements were used by the IEA to create an index of emphasis on academic success. Values on the index ranged from 'very high' for the highest values to a 'medium emphasis' for the lowest values.

Figure 10.2 compares the school emphasis on academic success by school grouping. Patterns for public and independent schools were very different. At least 70 per cent of learners attended public schools (both fee-paying and no-fee) that placed a medium emphasis on academic success (the lowest category). None of the learners at no-fee schools were in learning environments where a 'very high' emphasis was placed on academic success. Less than one per cent of learners that attended fee-paying schools were in the top category. By comparison, 23 per cent of learners in independent schools benefited from a very high emphasis on academic success that was in place at the school and only 35 per cent of learners were in schools where a medium emphasis on academic success was in place.

A comparison of the schooling environment

Figure 10.2: Percentage of learners attending schools that place emphasis on academic success by school type, 2015

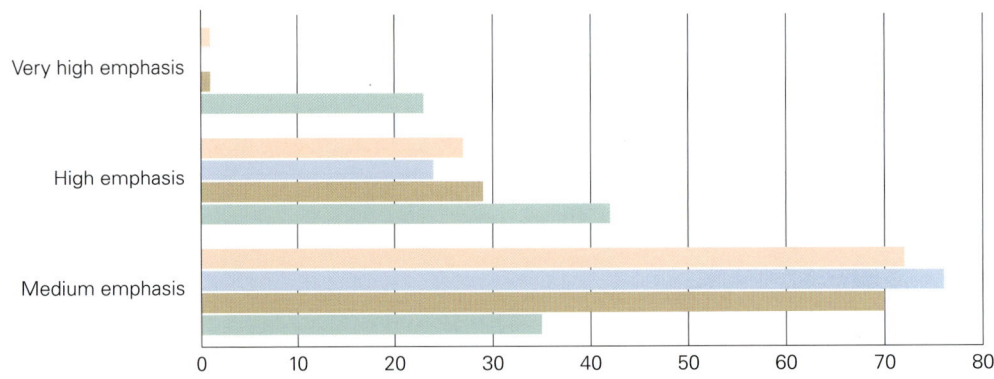

	Medium emphasis	High emphasis	Very high emphasis
National	72	27	1
Public (No-fee)	76	24	0
Public (Fee-paying)	70	29	1
Independent	35	42	23

10.3   Challenges facing teachers

An index and scale called 'challenges facing teachers' was created based on the extent to which mathematics and science teachers agreed with eight statements in the mathematics and science teacher questionnaires. These statements covered agreement with having too large class sizes, too much material to cover in class, too many teaching hours, too many administrative tasks, too much pressure from parents, the need for more time to prepare for class and to assist individual learners, and having difficulty in keeping up with curriculum changes. The scale index ranged from 'few' to 'many' challenges. Since the TIMSS sample is only generalisable at the learner level, Table 10.1 presents the percentage of learners in relation to both the mathematics and science teachers' responses. Nationally, 72 per cent of learners were taught by mathematics teachers who faced 'some' or 'many' challenges, while 68 per cent of learners were taught by science teachers who faced 'some' or 'many' challenges. None of the learners in independent schools were taught by teachers who experienced 'many' challenges. Challenges were more prevalent in public schools and highest in no-fee schools.

Table 10.1: Percentage of learners taught by mathematics and science teachers who experienced challenges by school type, 2015

School status		Mathematics teachers (SE)	Science teachers (SE)
National	Few challenges	28 (3.1)	32 (3.4)
	Some challenges	60 (3.5)	55 (3.2)
	Many challenges	12 (2.5)	13 (2.7)
Public (No-fee)	Few challenges	22 (3.6)	25 (3.7)
	Some challenges	65 (4.2)	60 (4.0)
	Many challenges	14 (3.1)	15 (3.7)
Public (Fee-paying)	Few challenges	36 (6.5)	37 (7.3)
	Some challenges	54 (6.9)	51 (6.5)
	Many challenges	10 (4.9)	12 (4.8)
Independent	Few challenges	70 (8.9)	90 (4.8)
	Some challenges	30 (8.9)	10 (4.8)

Figure 10.3 depicts the percentage of learners taught by mathematics and science teachers who 'agree a lot' with the statements that are described in the graph. Limited time to assist individual learners affected more than two-thirds of the learners (72 per cent and 69 per cent of learners taught by mathematics and science teachers respectively). More than half of the learners were affected by too crowded classrooms in mathematics (54 per cent) and science classes (55 per cent).

Figure 10.3: Percentage of learners affected based on mathematics and science teachers 'agree a lot' with the statement, 2015

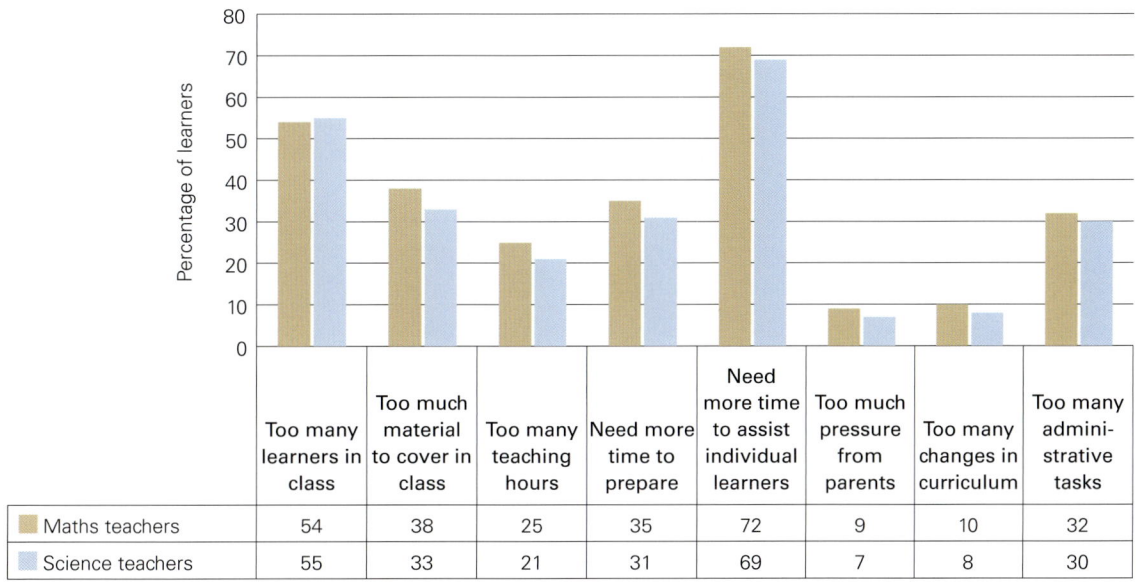

	Too many learners in class	Too much material to cover in class	Too many teaching hours	Need more time to prepare	Need more time to assist individual learners	Too much pressure from parents	Too many changes in curriculum	Too many administrative tasks
Maths teachers	54	38	25	35	72	9	10	32
Science teachers	55	33	21	31	69	7	8	30

10.4 School discipline

School principals were asked 11 questions about Grade 9 learners at their school and their responses were used to create a school discipline problems scale and index. Questions covered absenteeism, arriving late at school, classroom disturbances, cheating, profanities, vandalism, theft, intimidation, and physical injury to teaching staff. The values on the index ranged from 'hardly any' problems to 'moderate to severe' problems. Reports of discipline and safety followed the same pattern as other school climate results reported so far. Nationally, 34 per cent of learners attended schools where discipline problems were moderate to severe. In no-fee and fee-paying schools, the percentage was 39 per cent and 28 per cent respectively. Less than five per cent of learners attended independent schools where discipline problems were moderate to severe.

A comparison of the schooling environment

Figure 10.4: Percentage of learners attending schools with discipline problems by school type, 2015

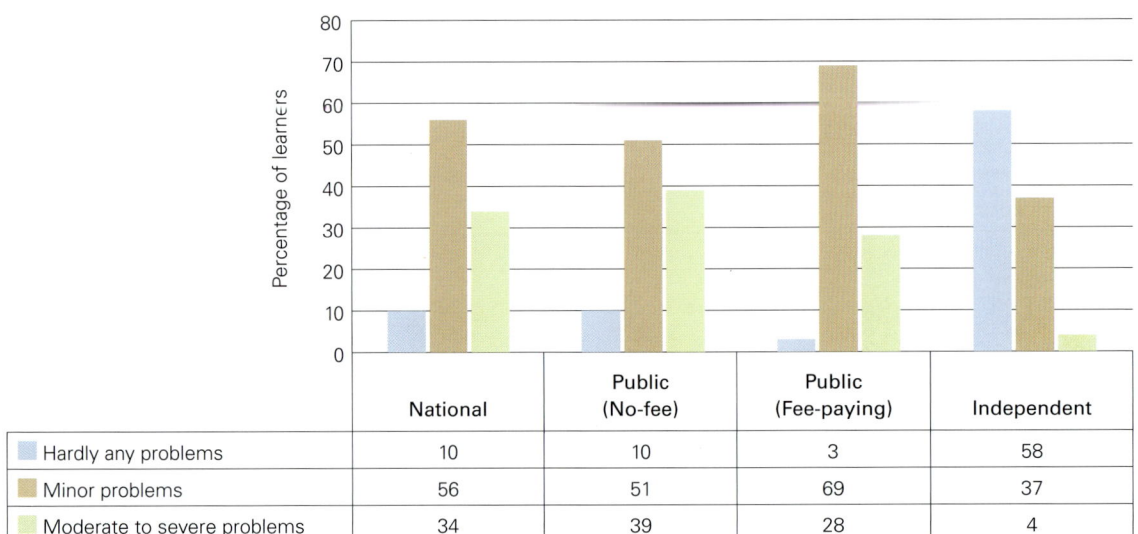

	National	Public (No-fee)	Public (Fee-paying)	Independent
Hardly any problems	10	10	3	58
Minor problems	56	51	69	37
Moderate to severe problems	34	39	28	4

Grade 9 learners were asked nine questions on the frequency and type of bullying that they experienced. These questions covered direct and indirect forms of bullying. Direct forms of bullying include both physical and verbal forms. Indirect bullying is relational and includes social exclusion and gossiping. Figure 10.5 shows patterns of bullying for learners who reported being victims at least once a week. The percentages presented in Figure 10.5 were calculated by using the number of learners who experienced bullying at least once a week out of the total number of learners who experienced bullying. The national results indicate that at least 25 per cent of learners were victims of each of the nine forms of bullying on a weekly basis. Learners in no-fee schools were more likely to be victims. At least 30 per cent were victims of each form of bullying on a weekly basis. More than 50 per cent of learners in no-fee schools reported that they were made fun of or called names at least once a week and more than 40 per cent were victims of theft on a weekly basis.

The most widespread forms of being bullied in fee-paying and independent schools were being victims of theft and name calling. The percentage of learners who were victims of cyber bullying in independent schools (posted embarrassing things about me online) was lower than in fee-paying and no-fee school groupings.

Figure 10.5: Percentage of learners who were bullied at least once a week by forms of bullying and school type, 2015

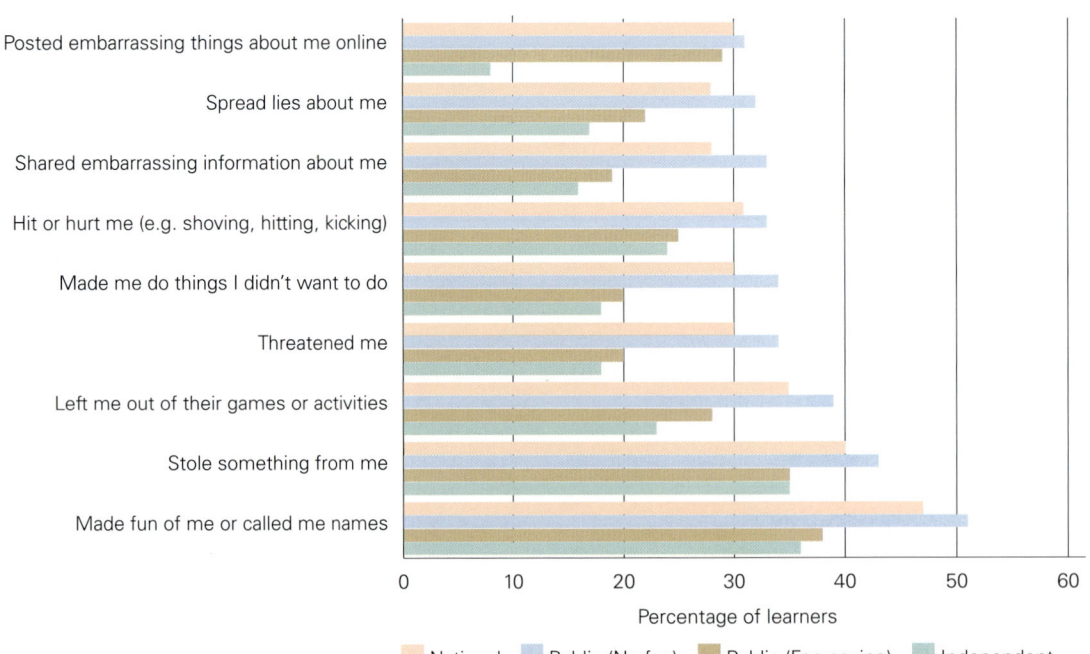

Cycles of bullying are more difficult to break where a high percentage of learners are both bullies (culprits) and victims of bullying, so understanding these patterns is important for improving overall safety at schools.

In addition to questions about frequency of being bullied, Grade 9 learners in the South African study were also asked how often they were the instigators of bullying. Cycles of bullying are more difficult to break where a high percentage of learners are both bullies (culprits) and victims of bullying, so understanding these patterns is important for improving overall safety at schools. Figure 10.6 summarises responses to questions about being perpetrators of bullying. The percentages presented in Figure 10.6 were calculated by using the number of learners who were perpetrators of bullying at least once a week out of the total number of perpetrators of bullying. Again, national results indicate that at least 25 per cent of learners were perpetrators on a weekly basis. Learners in no-fee schools bullied others the most frequently. Different forms of bullying were common but the most recurrent forms were making fun of others, leaving others out of games and making other learners do things that they did not want to do. Whereas patterns of bullying in fee-paying and independent schools were similar, there was a noticeable difference in the perpetrator data. The percentage of learners who participated in bullying was much lower in independent schools. On six of the nine indicators, less than 11 per cent of learners stated that they were perpetrators at least weekly. The fact that this is self-reported data raises the question of whether perpetrators would supply accurate data about their misconduct. In addition, there is a tendency to underreport episodes of assault in schools (Burton & Leoschut, 2013). However, these results provide a sense of general trends.

Figure 10.6: Percentage of learners who were perpetrators at least once a week by forms of bullying and school type, 2015

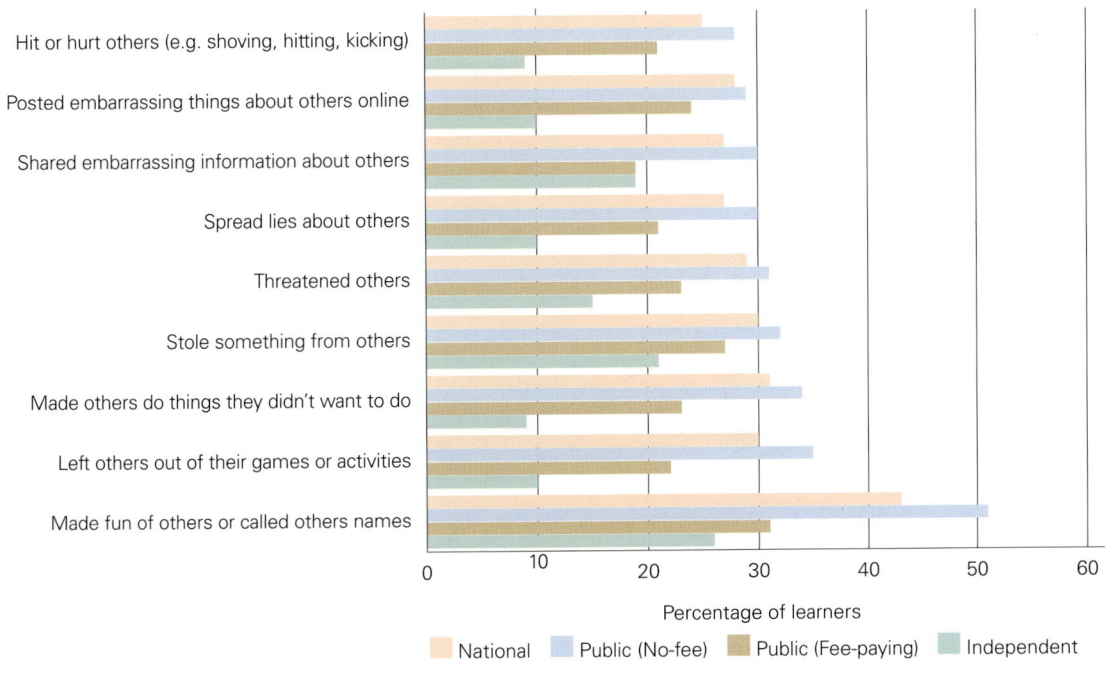

PART D

11. Teachers and classroom instruction

Collaboration among teachers is an important part of school life. Teachers benefit from interacting with each other to ensure consistency and continuity in curriculum coverage. Teachers also need to be at school and on time for instruction to happen. Although teachers are entitled to take leave as part of their employment conditions, absenteeism may exceed what is prescribed and for a variety of reasons. Absences can be due to participation in professional training, attending to official business, illness and family responsibility (Reddy et al., 2010).

11.1 Teacher interaction

As mentioned earlier, mathematics and science teachers' responses to the questionnaires are not nationally representative in TIMSS, but the TIMSS sample is representative on the learner level, therefore responses of principals and teachers are given in relation to the number of learners involved. Teacher reports about their levels of interaction with colleagues are shown in Figure 11.1. The graph presents the percentage of learners who received instruction from mathematics teachers who interacted 'very often' on a list of activities. For mathematics, learners from independent schools were taught by teachers who interacted the most frequently in terms of discussing topics, planning lessons, sharing ideas and following the curriculum. In no-fee schools, 37 per cent of learners were taught by teachers who discussed how to teach a particular topic on a regular basis. This was the most frequent form of teacher interaction in no-fee schools. For learners in fee-paying schools, the most common form of interaction was teachers who worked as a group to implement the curriculum. Working with teachers from other grades to ensure continuity was one of the least practised activities across all types of schools.

Figure 11.1: Percentage of learners taught by mathematics teachers who interacted 'very often' by school type, 2015

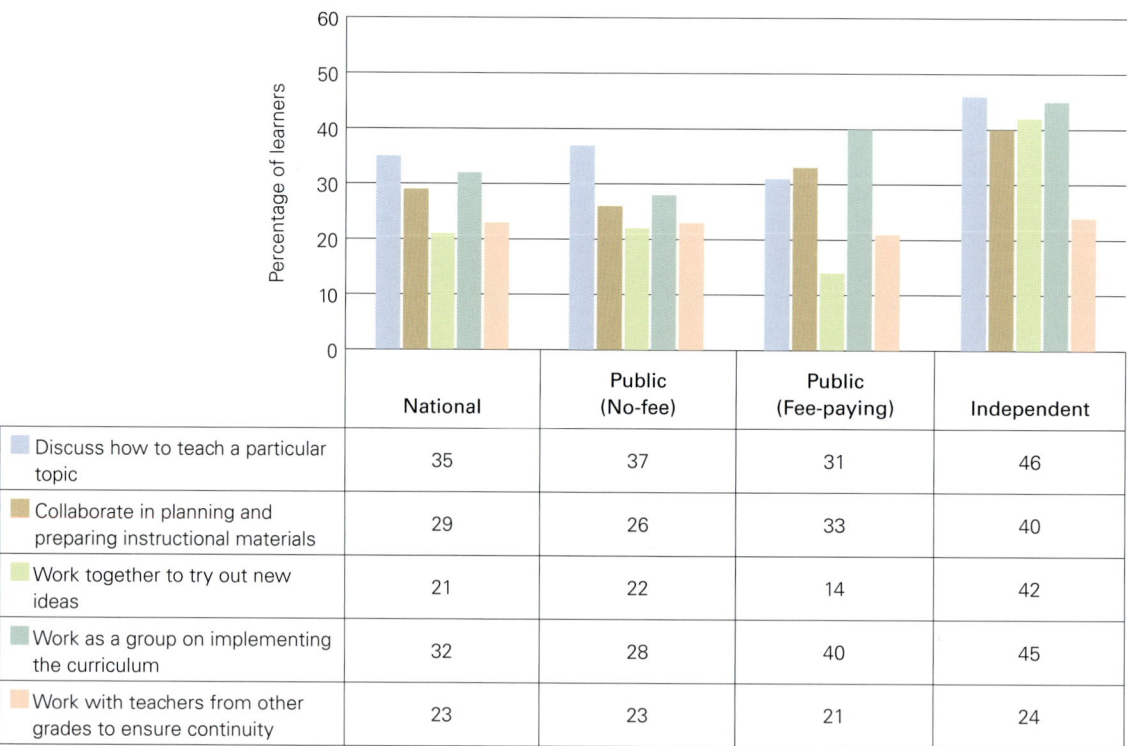

	National	Public (No-fee)	Public (Fee-paying)	Independent
Discuss how to teach a particular topic	35	37	31	46
Collaborate in planning and preparing instructional materials	29	26	33	40
Work together to try out new ideas	21	22	14	42
Work as a group on implementing the curriculum	32	28	40	45
Work with teachers from other grades to ensure continuity	23	23	21	24

The percentage of learners taught by science teachers who collaborated regularly was lower than the percentage reported for mathematics teachers. Less than one-quarter of learners in no-fee schools were taught by science teachers who reported interacting with their peers on any of the listed areas. Learners in fee-paying schools received instruction from teachers who interacted more often but again learners in independent schools benefited from more regular teacher engagement. In every schooling environment the most common reason for working together was to ensure that the curriculum was implemented.

Figure 11.2: Percentage of learners taught by science teachers who interacted 'very often' by school type, 2015

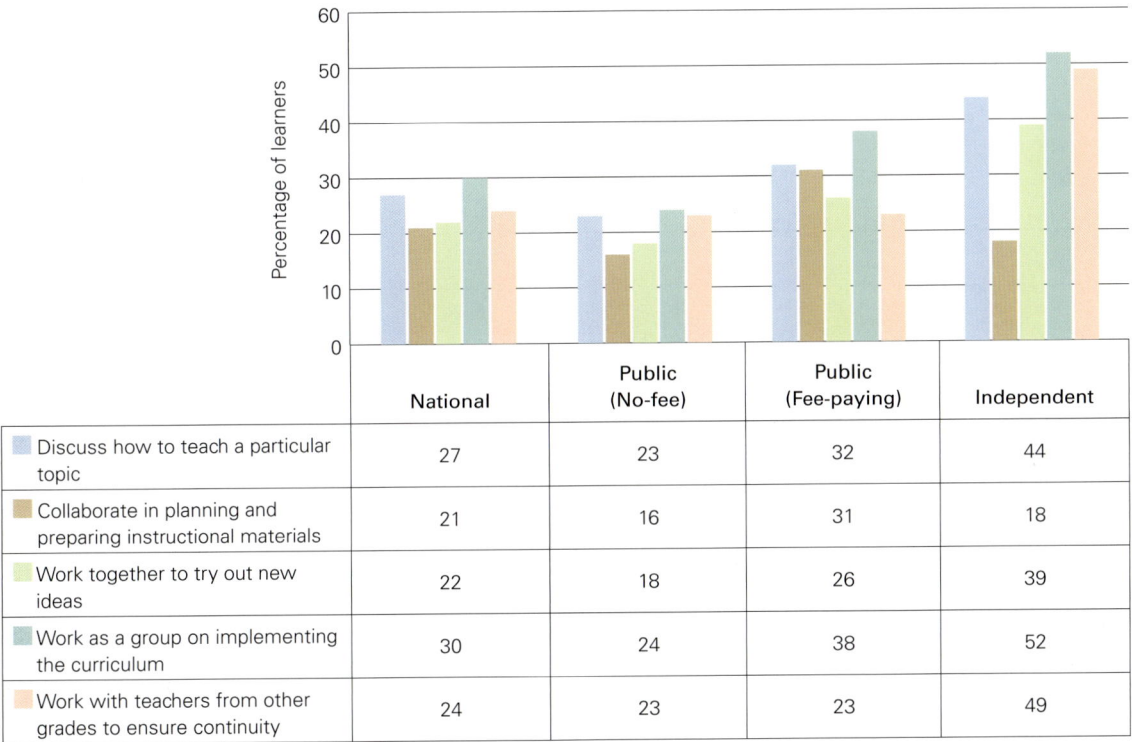

	National	Public (No-fee)	Public (Fee-paying)	Independent
Discuss how to teach a particular topic	27	23	32	44
Collaborate in planning and preparing instructional materials	21	16	31	18
Work together to try out new ideas	22	18	26	39
Work as a group on implementing the curriculum	30	24	38	52
Work with teachers from other grades to ensure continuity	24	23	23	49

11.2   Teacher vacancies

One-quarter of learners attended schools where principals reported that it was very difficult to fill vacancies for mathematics teachers (Figure 11.3). School principals in public schools had the greatest difficulty filling these positions. Thirty-one per cent of learners attended no-fee schools where the principal reported that it was very difficult to fill vacancies, compared to 16 per cent of learners in fee-paying schools and three per cent of learners in independent schools. Moreover, 60 per cent of learners attended independent schools where the principal reported that they had no vacancies for mathematics teachers.

A comparison of the schooling environment

Figure 11.3: Percentage of learners attending schools that have difficulty filling mathematics positions by school type, 2015

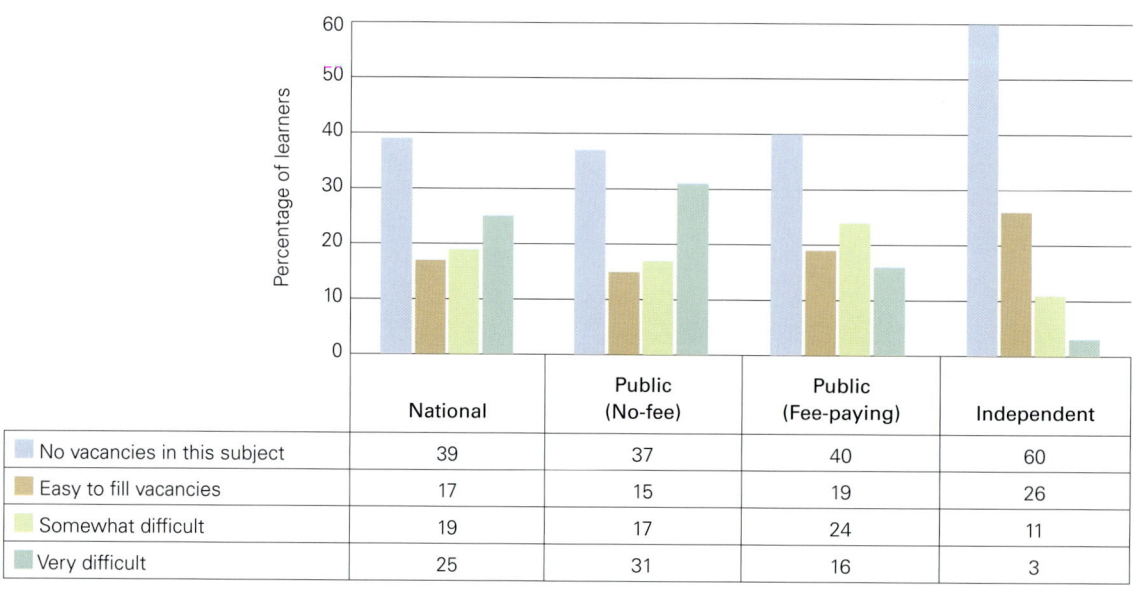

	National	Public (No-fee)	Public (Fee-paying)	Independent
No vacancies in this subject	39	37	40	60
Easy to fill vacancies	17	15	19	26
Somewhat difficult	19	17	24	11
Very difficult	25	31	16	3

Figure 11.4 shows that 24 per cent of learners attended schools where principals reported that it was very difficult to fill vacancies for science teachers. Twenty-nine per cent of learners attended no-fee schools where the principal reported that it was very difficult to fill vacancies, compared to 15 per cent of learners in fee-paying schools and 22 per cent of learners in independent schools.

Figure 11.4: Percentage of learners attending schools that have difficulty filling science positions by school type, 2015

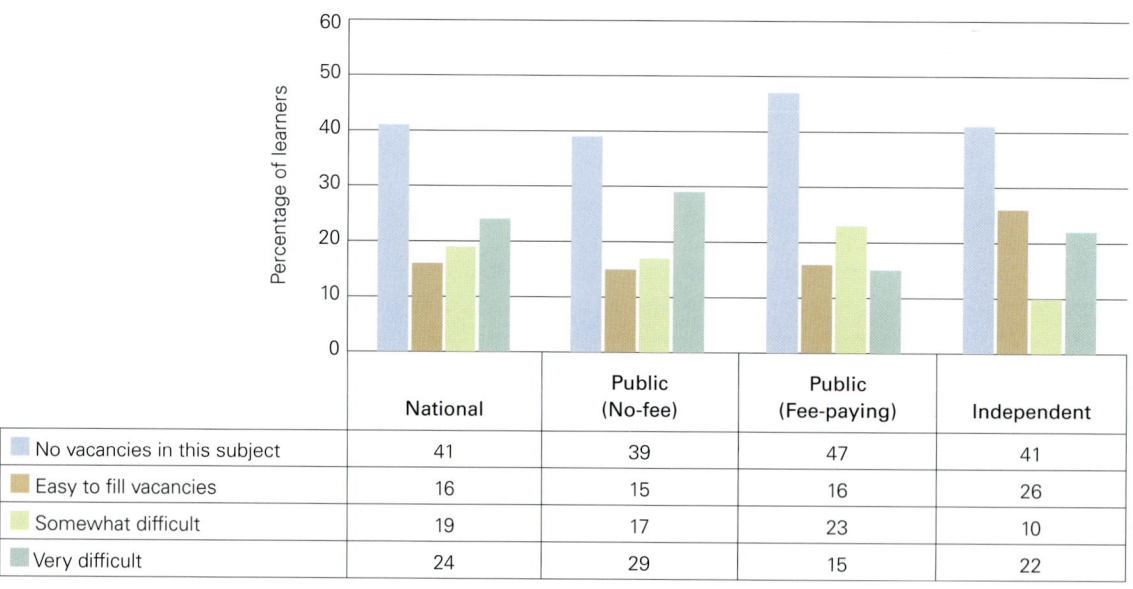

	National	Public (No-fee)	Public (Fee-paying)	Independent
No vacancies in this subject	41	39	47	41
Easy to fill vacancies	16	15	16	26
Somewhat difficult	19	17	23	10
Very difficult	24	29	15	22

11.3 Teacher absenteeism and arriving late

School principals were also asked to rate how seriously they viewed teacher absenteeism and arriving late. These responses are compared across types of schools in Figures 11.5 and 11.6. Twenty-seven per cent of Grade 9 learners attended schools where principals did not view teacher absenteeism as a problem. Only five per cent of learners attended schools where principals viewed absenteeism as a serious problem. Teacher absenteeism was less of an issue in independent schools – only three per cent of learners were affected.

Figure 11.5: Percentage of learners attending schools with teacher absenteeism problems by school type, 2015

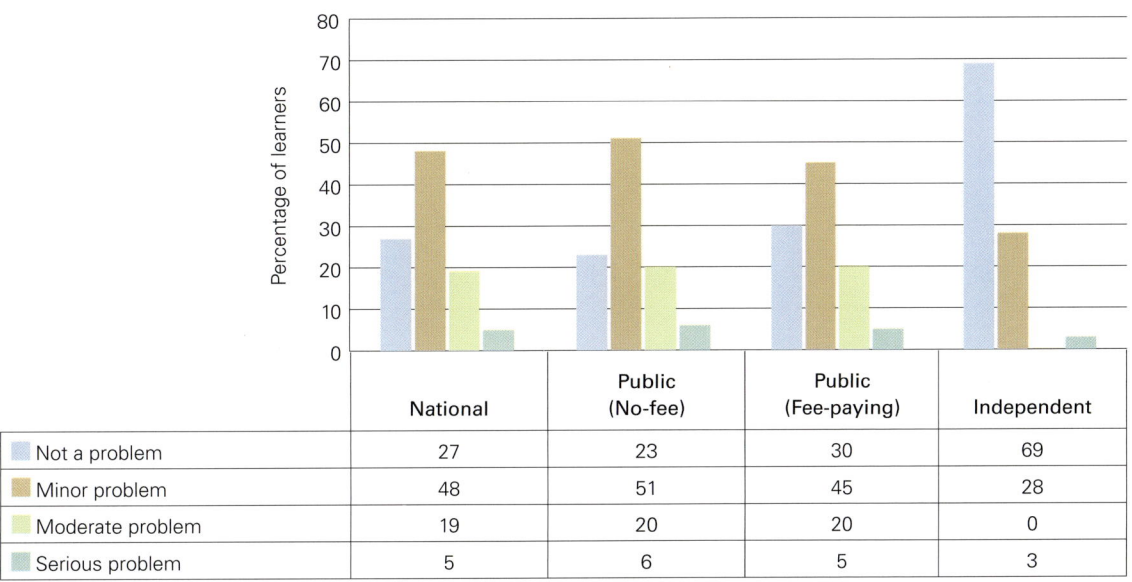

	National	Public (No-fee)	Public (Fee-paying)	Independent
Not a problem	27	23	30	69
Minor problem	48	51	45	28
Moderate problem	19	20	20	0
Serious problem	5	6	5	3

Like teacher absenteeism, few principals reported late arrivals as a problematic occurrence in schools. Five per cent of Grade 9 learners attended schools where principals viewed teacher late coming as serious. For 33 per cent of no-fee school learners, principals did not view teacher punctuality as a problem. The equivalent response was 44 per cent for learners in fee-paying schools and 72 per cent for learners in independent schools.

Figure 11.6: Percentage of learners attending schools where teachers arrive late by school type, 2015

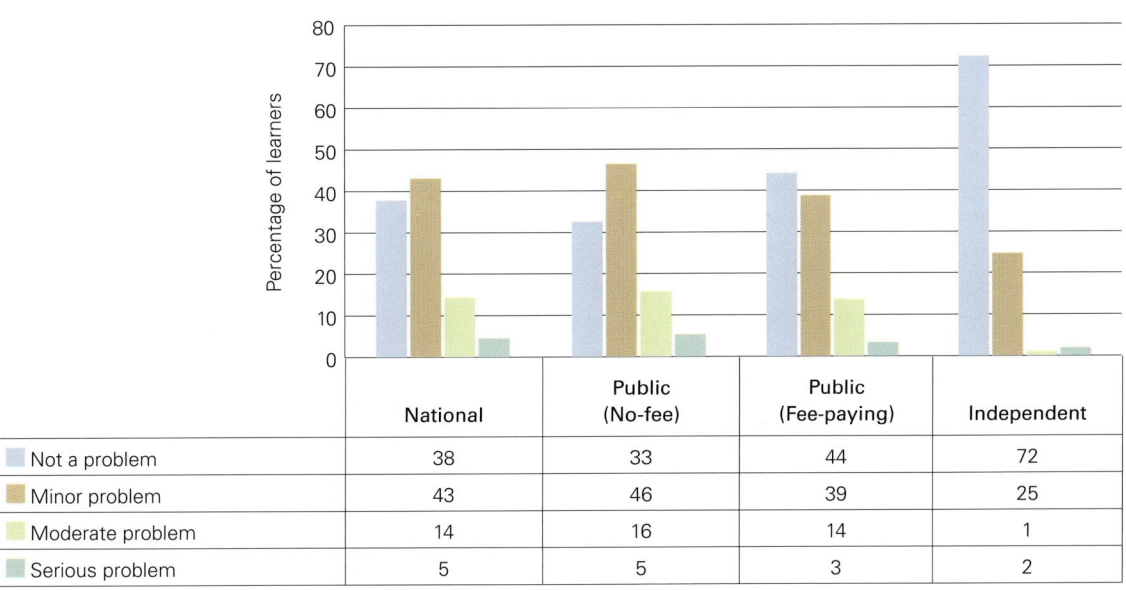

	National	Public (No-fee)	Public (Fee-paying)	Independent
Not a problem	38	33	44	72
Minor problem	43	46	39	25
Moderate problem	14	16	14	1
Serious problem	5	5	3	2

PART D

A comparison of the schooling environment

Learners were asked how often they were absent from school. Two-thirds of Grade 9 learners responded that they were 'never' or 'almost never' absent from school (Figure 11.7). Responses to questions on absenteeism were similar across schooling environments.

Figure 11.7: Learner absenteeism by school type, 2015

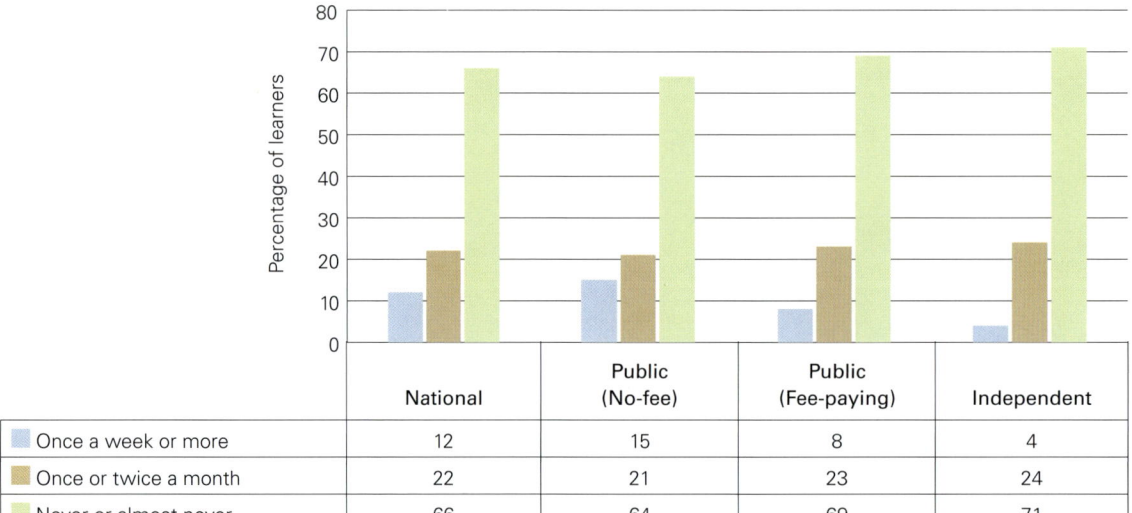

	National	Public (No-fee)	Public (Fee-paying)	Independent
Once a week or more	12	15	8	4
Once or twice a month	22	21	23	24
Never or almost never	66	64	69	71

Section summary

This section showed that there were provincial differences in the provision of pedagogical resources such as textbooks, with the same provinces having the most limited distribution of both mathematics and science textbooks. Textbook ownership was associated with average test scores, particularly in no-fee schools. Apart from restricted textbook access, library and laboratory facilities were most limited in no-fee schools. Resources in and of themselves will not make a difference in achievement if they are not used correctly and if the learning environment is not conducive. In addition to the resource shortages at schools, learners from public schools were at a severe disadvantage in every aspect of school climate reported. No-fee schools were particularly vulnerable to a poor school climate. Learners attending no-fee schools were exposed to a lower emphasis on academic success, teachers who were less satisfied with their jobs and principals who reported more widespread discipline problems. There was, however, a high sense of belonging in no-fee schools. Bullying behaviour was widespread in all schools but again, most common in no-fee schools. Significantly, learners were involved in bullying others more frequently in public schools when compared to independent schools. Teachers interviewed in TIMSS 2015 showed a willingness to collaborate with other staff in order to improve teaching and learning. Teachers in independent schools seemed to interact with each other more systematically. Filling teacher vacancies was far more difficult in no-fee schools. Teacher absenteeism and late arrivals were more common in public schools. There was a greater emphasis placed on punctuality in independent schools.

PART **E**

THE SCHOOL'S INFLUENCE ON MATHEMATICS ACHIEVEMENT

The school's influence on mathematics achievement

12. School effectiveness in South Africa

In the introduction to this report, we described the three approaches that would be used to discuss educational issues related to the TIMSS 2015 results. The first approach provided results of descriptive analyses. It showed trends in TIMSS performance across time and what was happening in learners' home and schooling environments. The second approach is the focus of this section. It is concerned with why things are happening as they do and is based on analysis of relationships between variables. It investigates how learner and school characteristics are associated with achievement. We focus on the mathematics results to demonstrate how inferential statistics can deepen our interpretation of the results.

12.1 Why focus on school effectiveness in South African educational policy?

South African learners experience their education in the context of classrooms and schools. They are assigned to classrooms and these classrooms are situated within the same school. The previous sections showed that learners come to their education with considerable differences in their personal characteristics (such as gender, age and attitudes) and their educational experiences (e.g. support for learning outside of schools). Learners' educational outcomes are also associated with characteristics of their families (e.g. SES and type of residence). There are many interesting outcomes that can be used to relate learners, schools and their education. In this section, we focus on perhaps one of the most important and obvious outcomes: academic achievement as measured by a TIMSS assessment in mathematics. Because the results of mathematics and science scores were very closely correlated, we only report on the analysis of the mathematics test results in the discussion that follows. In general, measures of child and family characteristics are less amenable to policy intervention than are measures of school characteristics. For this reason, the focus of the discussion will be on school effectiveness.

Figure 12.1: A conceptual framework for school effectiveness

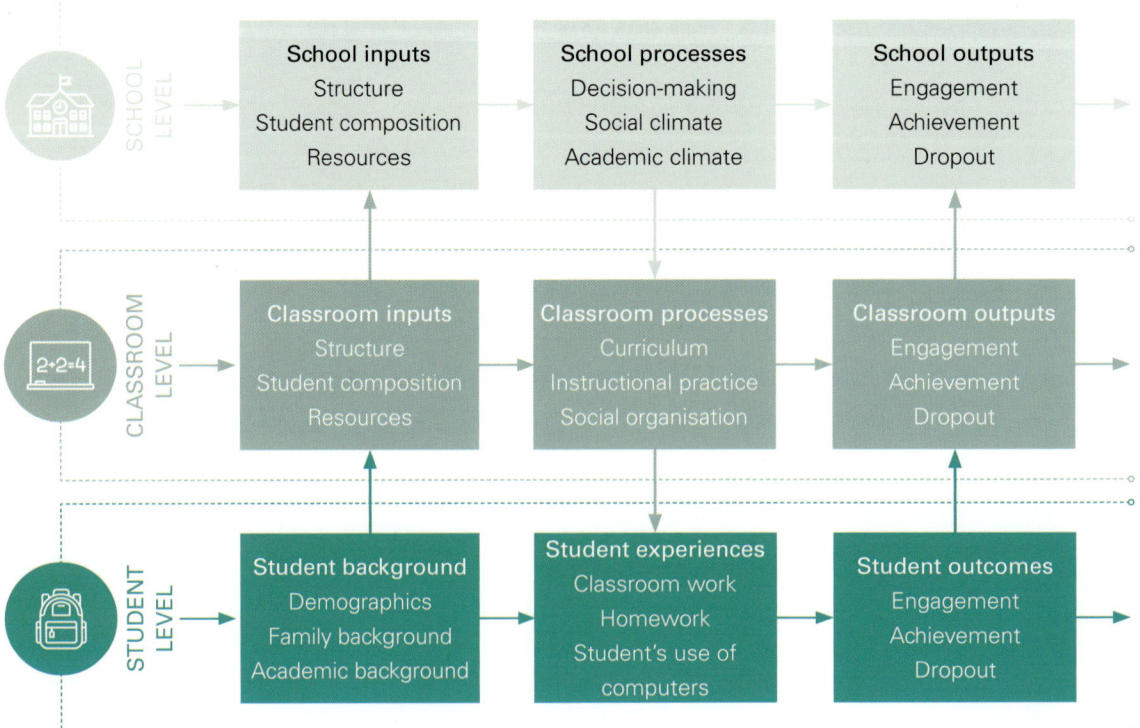

Source: (Rumberger. & Palardy, 2004)

School effectiveness research was in many ways a response to the Coleman Report in the United States and the 1971 Plowden Report on children in England and Wales (Coleman et al., 1966; Peaker, 1971). Findings of these reports implied that there was a limit to what a school system could do to reverse persistent social disadvantage. This sparked off decades of empirical research to prove the influence of schools on academic achievement. Much of the criticism was directed at the framework and method that was used to measure and analyse school effects. As mentioned, education occurs within a context and due to its nested structure, appropriate analytical techniques need to be employed. A conceptual framework of school effectiveness needs to take into account the hierarchical nature of education data. Three components are typically included (see Figure 12.1). The first component is the inputs to schooling which would include the human and physical resources provided to a school by the national education department. The second component is focused on the educational processes within a school (for example how inputs are used, the climate of the school) and the final component is the outcome of schooling, which is generally measured by learner achievement.

Beyond describing individuals, it is also important to describe the context in which learners experience their education. Characteristics of schools can include the school structural characteristics (e.g. no-fee, fee-paying or independent school), the types of learners enrolled at the school (average SES of learners or the percentage of learners who are over-age for their grade, for example), or those that describe basic characteristics of school organisation (such as the physical and human resources on which the school may draw or the type of climate within the school). An important feature of the school-level variables is that they do not vary among individual learners within the school. Learners in the same school are exposed to the same conditions that are represented by these school variables. Learners in the same school have access to the same resources and are exposed to the same organisational setting. In general, measures of this sort are more likely to be amenable to policy intervention.

Questions that involve evaluating how particular educational policies, which impact on schooling, influence student achievement, are called multilevel questions. This is because we want to estimate the relationship between variables describing schools on the one hand and student outcomes, such as individual achievement, on the other. This type of inquiry also falls within a broader category of educational research called "school effectiveness studies".

12.2 Which questions are to be addressed for the TIMSS 2015 Grade 9 study?

Three important insights emerged from the descriptive analysis presented earlier in this report:

1. The backgrounds of learners attending public and independent schools are highly uneven, with more affluent parents sending their children to fee-paying schools and independent schools and learners from poor households attending the no-fee schools. Learners from resource-rich environments tend to have access to greater support for their education outside of school. They are also more fluent in the LoLT, which has been shown as integral to success in high-stakes assessments.

2. The distribution of educational resources in South African schools continues to be highly uneven, with the far more numerous no-fee schools having access to fewer resources to support learning. Much-needed additional funding for education can come from voluntary support from parents for their children's education, but widespread poverty limits the direct contributions that can be made by many low-income households.

3. Learners attending better-resourced schools also benefit from a more conducive educational climate, with fewer challenges to interfere with teaching and learning, where discipline is the norm and academic excellence is encouraged. Learners in poor schools face a less favourable climate on a daily basis, over and above the resource shortages at home and at school.

The school's influence on mathematics achievement

Taken together, these descriptive results suggest that the research questions in this context should focus on the school structure, access to educational resources and the type of climate to which learners are exposed in South African schools. We also need to understand the level of inequality that exists between schools before explaining what school factors are responsible for the differences. Learner contextual factors are considered so that their association with achievement is taken into account before focusing on school factors. We construct the following related research questions:

Question 1: How do South African secondary schools vary in terms of their average Grade 9 mathematics achievement?

Question 2: How are learner contextual factors related to mathematics achievement of Grade 9 learners in South Africa?

Question 3: How are a school's structure, resources and climate associated with South African Grade 9 mathematics achievement once learner contextual factors are accounted for?

12.3   What method was used to answer the research questions?

Multilevel analysis is a statistical technique that has been widely used in the social sciences when data have a nested structure, learners within classrooms and classrooms within schools (Hox, 2010; Raudenbush & Bryk, 2002; Snijders & Bosker, 1999). The multilevel analysis for this report was conducted using a software package called Hierarchical Linear Modelling (HLM) that was developed by Raudenbush and his colleagues (Raudenbush, Bryk & Congdon, 2013). The TIMSS 2015 sample consisted of 12 514 learners from 292 schools as shown in Figure 12.2. In each school, an intact classroom of Grade 9 learners was assessed[13]. In addition to having data that are hierarchical (Grade 9 learners who are grouped within schools), the research questions are also hierarchical in nature. One of the advantages of using multilevel analysis is that it separates the part of learner achievement that can be explained by learner characteristics and the part that can be explained by school factors. Since school effectiveness is the focus of the current analysis, an additional advantage is that it is possible to isolate the effect of school factors after controlling for certain learner contextual factors.

Figure 12.2: The number of learners and schools in TIMSS 2015

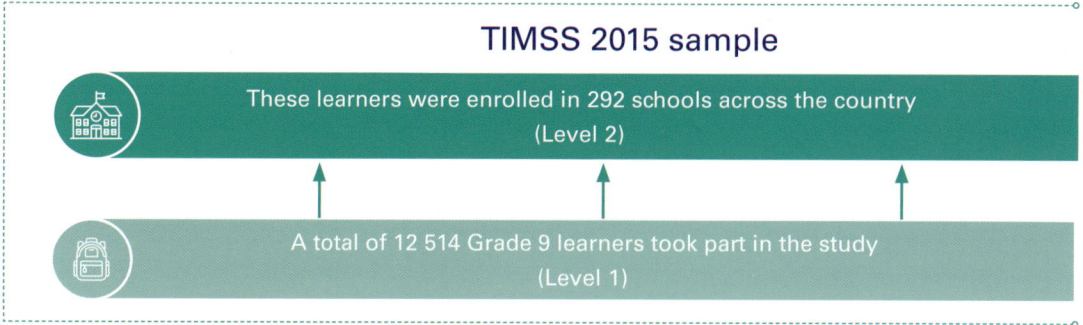

There were three steps involved in analysing the data to address the three research questions that were listed.

---

[13] Because the TIMSS design samples intact classes, it was not possible to analyse differences in achievement between classes at the same school.

The first step involved estimating a one-way ANOVA model. This required selecting the outcome variable (TIMSS mathematics achievement scores) and partitioning the total variance in the outcome into its within-school (level 1) and its between-school (level 2) components. The most important information from this model is the intraclass correlation coefficient (ICC). The ICC indicates the proportion of the total variance in the outcome variable that lies systematically between and within schools. The ICC is important because it is a measure of inequality between schools; a high ICC would indicate that there is considerable inequality between schools in South Africa. By adding school factors to the model (as shown in section 12.4.3 below) the variance between schools is reduced. The amount that it is reduced depends on how well the school variables explain differences between schools.

In the second step, only level 1 (learner) variables were included. Learners vary in many different ways, such as their gender, SES and educational background. Before selecting school variables to explain achievement differences between schools, this interim step involved assessing the strength of the relationship between learner achievement scores and learner background characteristics. Since the model focused on modelling the intercept; within-school independent variables were fixed. The results presented in section 12.4.2 below are based on the final HLM model after school factors are included.

The main part of the analyses for exploring multilevel research questions was accomplished with variables at the school level (step 3 of the analysis). School effectiveness was defined as average mathematics achievement after adjusting for student background. How characteristics of schools influenced the mathematics outcomes of Grade 9 learners who attend these schools was explored here. This is the essence of the third multilevel educational question described earlier in this section. The size of the HLM coefficients associated with each school-level variable, along with its level of statistical significance, indicated which school characteristics are significantly associated with effectiveness. Variables were added step by step. In the first model, only school structure variables were used. In the second model, both school structure and school resources variables were included. In the final model, school structure, school resources and school climate factors were added.

12.4 What do these results mean?

12.4.1 The intraclass correlation coefficient (ICC)

Figure 12.3 presents the ICC calculation based on the TIMSS 2015 Grade 9 mathematics test scores. The decomposition of variance into its between- and within-group components shows that 61 per cent of total variance for Grade 9 mathematics occurred between schools and 39 per cent existed between learners within schools. From 2011 to 2015 there was a decrease in between-school variance from 64 per cent to 61 per cent, which indicates that the inequality gap is narrowed slightly. Although ICCs in developing countries are typically higher than in industrialised countries (Lee et al., 2005; Lee & Zuze, 2011), the results for South Africa point to a particularly high level of inequality across schools in the education system. As a comparison, the within-school variation for learners in Finland who took part in the Programme for International Student Assessment (PISA) in 2012 was 92.5 per cent (OECD, 2013a). Only eight per cent of variation was between schools. In such an equitable system, learners are virtually guaranteed the same quality of schooling, irrespective of the school that they attend. Closer to home, the ICC for Botswana for TIMSS 2011 was 19 per cent compared to 64 per cent for South African Grade 9 learners. This suggests that there has been a slight improvement since 2011 but that inequality in South African secondary schools exceeds that of other education systems.

PART E

The school's influence on mathematics achievement

Figure 12.3: The ICC for Grade 9 mathematics, 2015

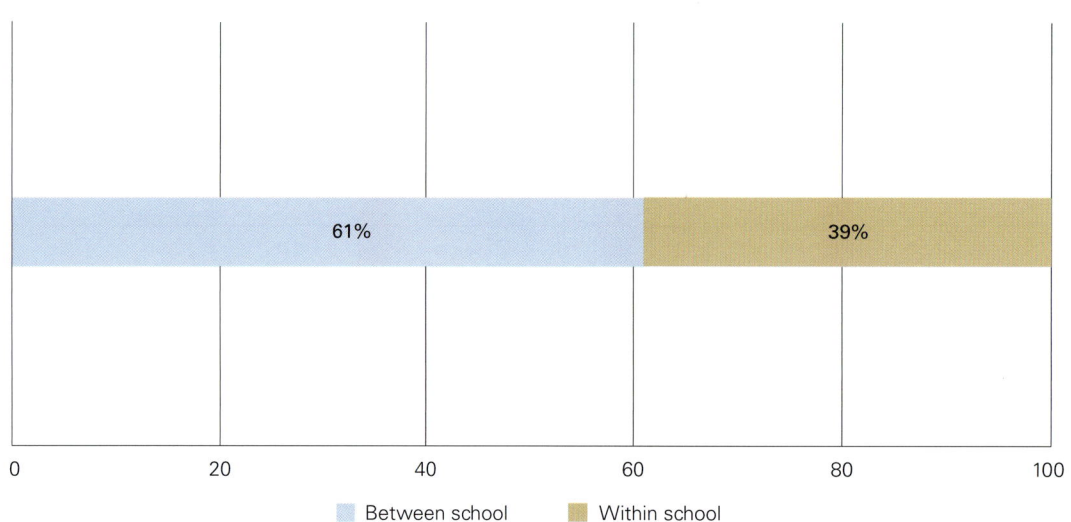

12.4.2 *Learner contextual factors and TIMSS mathematics achievement*

In relating family background to TIMSS achievement, we took the following learner characteristics into consideration: learner SES, which included the availability of 16 assets in the home (details provided in section 6 of the current report), the age of learners, the gender of learners, whether learners spoke the language of the test frequently (always or almost always) and whether learners were ever victims of bullying (either monthly or weekly).

Table 12.1 summarises the results of the multilevel regression analysis of learner characteristics and achievement (the second research question). Older learners, learners who were victims of bullying and girls were at a disadvantage when these learner characteristics were analysed together. Each additional year in learner age was associated with a 16 point decline in TIMSS mathematics scores. Learners who were victims of bullying (either weekly or monthly) achieved scores which were six points lower than those of learners who were never bullied. Previously we noted that there were no gender differences when average performance of learners was compared. However, when other learner characteristics are set aside, girls achieved significantly lower test scores than boys. Predictably, learners of a higher SES and learners who spoke the language of the test frequently outside of school achieved higher test scores. The advantage of language fluency remained positive and significant over and above the influence of SES. This clearly shows that the importance of language fluency goes beyond a learner's socioeconomic circumstances.

Table 12.1: Learner contextual factors and TIMSS mathematics achievement, 2015

Intercept	384.46***
Socioeconomic status	3.11**
Age	-16.19***
Female	-11.37***
Frequency of speaking the test language	14.80***
Bullying	-6.08***
Random effects	
Mean achievement	3 636.91***
Rij	2 858.25
Reliability of Ordinary Least Square regression-coefficient estimates	
Mean achievement	0.98

*, **, *** *indicate significance at 10%, 5% and 1% levels.*

Physical resources exerted independent and positive effects on school average achievement because this suggests that resources really matter for educational quality.

12.4.3 School factors and TIMSS mathematics achievement

In Table 12.2 the results of the analysis addressing the third research question related to school factors and TIMSS achievement are shown. Learner characteristics were taken into account in running this analysis and therefore are not repeated in Table 12.2. Our third question focused on particular school features of educational policy – namely, the structure, resourcing and climate of schooling. Throughout this report, we have considered three types of schooling environments: no-fee schools, fee-paying schools and independent schools. To an extent, these environments represent the type of physical and human resources on which a school may draw because of the financial support provided to schools where tuition fees are charged. Many studies of education in the developing world have found that resources really matter for achievement (Lee et al., 2005; Zuze & Leibbrandt, 2011). In addition to the resources represented by the structure of schooling, we also explicitly included variables related to the availability and shortage of physical resources in the second model shown below.

Our findings related to resources are both heartening and discouraging. It is heartening to find that if schools have more physical resources (library facilities) and fewer resource shortages (materials to teach mathematics), then achievement is higher. Moreover, these resource effects persisted even when we took account of the type of school attended (no-fee, fee-paying or independent). This implies that the resource findings are real and not simply artefacts of the type of school learners attend. It is good news for policy that physical resources exerted independent and positive effects on school average achievement because this suggests that resources really matter for educational quality. However, the news about the school type and average achievement is not as good. Compared to no-fee schools, school average achievement was significantly higher in fee-paying schools and higher still in independent schools. Part of this school achievement gap was explained by the availability of physical resources. The strength of the relationship between school type and mathematics achievement reduced when physical resources were included in the analysis in model 2[14]. However, a far greater part of the achievement gap was explained by the school climate as discussed below.

The school climate was represented by a number of TIMSS indicators that captured the quality of the learning environment. These were: the school's emphasis on academic success, whether a school experienced disciplinary problems, whether a school was safe and orderly, frequency of bullying in schools and whether teachers felt that they faced challenges in the classroom. Higher values on these indexes represented a more positive climate. Bullying was included at the school level as well because it is a measure of school climate but also because the effect of bullying could vary significantly between schools as well as within schools.

The importance of school climate is very clear from this analysis. Not only did different dimensions of school climate contribute to higher school average achievement, but they explained the difference in average test scores between no-fee, fee-paying and independent schools. Moreover at schools where bullying was widespread, learners achieved lower average test scores, even when the resource levels of schools was accounted for. Creating a healthy school climate clearly requires far more than just improving the quantity and quality of resources available at a school. How to ensure that the organisational and professional conditions of the school support learning should remain a high educational priority for South African policy makers.

---

[14] This relationship is represented by the size of the coefficients in Table 12.2.

The school's influence on mathematics achievement

Table 12.2: School factors and TIMSS mathematics achievement, 2015

	Model 1: School structure	Model 2: School resources	Model 3: School climate[a]
Intercept	353.68***	351.86***	359.23***
School structure (Reference No-fee)			
Fee-paying	72.99***	66.73***	48.56***
Independent	118.89***	93.45***	44.96***
School resources			
Library		11.29*	11.16***
Shortage in mathematics material		15.45***	9.11**
School climate			
School emphasis on academic success			5.05***
School (few) discipline problems			6.37*
Safe and orderly schools			6.62**
Frequency of student bullying			-14.11***
Few challenges faced by teachers			9.88***
Random effects			
Mean achievement	1 995.77***	1 806.08***	1 308.36***
Rij	2 857.68	2 857.54	2 857.86
Reliability of Ordinary Least Square regression-coefficient estimates			
Mean achievement	0.96	0.96	0.95

*, **, *** *indicate significance at 10%, 5% and 1% levels.*
[a] *The final model was successful in explaining 64 per cent of variance or differences in mathematics achievement between schools.*

Section summary

Although inequality between South African schools is higher than elsewhere in the developing world, there have been slight improvements over time. The background of Grade 9 learners and TIMSS mathematics achievement are associated in a number of important but predictable ways. The role of language fluency stood out as making a difference, which will support the discussion that follows on national proficiency benchmarks. Schools with more resources to draw upon and better facilities devoted to education were at an advantage, but the climate of learning played a unique and significant role in TIMSS Grade 9 achievement that went beyond access to resources. Because our analyses make use of cross-sectional data (all TIMSS data are cross-sectional), our ability to draw strong causal inferences is not good. That is, it could as easily be the case that the most able learners are drawn to schools because they may draw on more resources or because these schools have a more conducive learning environment as the causal direction we have implied in our discussion – that more resources and better school climate result in higher achievement. Thus, our interpretation of the results here is positive, but modest at best.

PART F

SCIENCE CURRICULUM INSIGHTS FROM NATIONAL AND INTERNATIONAL BENCHMARKS

Science curriculum insights from national and international benchmarks

13. Science curriculum and national benchmarks

TIMSS uses the curriculum, broadly defined, as the major organising concept in considering how educational opportunities are provided to students and the factors that influence how students use these opportunities. The TIMSS Curriculum Model has three aspects: the intended curriculum, the implemented curriculum, and the attained curriculum. The TIMSS 2015 achievement results are summarised using IRT scaling and report mathematics achievement scores on a scale with a mean of 500 and a standard deviation of 100. The countries' average scores provide users of the data with information about how achievement compares among countries and whether scores are changing over time.

In order to extend the information for policy and curriculum reform, however, it is important to understand the science competencies associated with different locations within the range of scores on the achievement scales. These performance level descriptors describe what learners know and can do within the performance levels of knowledge and skills (Zieky, 2012).

In addition to describing TIMSS achievement by the IRT scaled score, TIMSS has created a set of international benchmarks to provide participating countries with comparable descriptions of what learners know and can do at different locations within the range of scores on the achievement scales. TIMSS defines four categories of benchmarks, namely: scores between 400 and 475 points are classified as achievement at a *low* level, scores between 475 and 550 points as achievement at an *intermediate* level, scores from 550 to 625 points as achievement at a *high* level and scores above 625 points as achievement at an *advanced* level[15].

In order to make the global assessment locally meaningful, we extended the analyses using Rasch techniques to create a natural benchmark scale of TIMSS performance. A comprehensive report on the methodology and results of this analysis is available on the TIMSS South Africa website (Scherman, Long, Coetzee & Abrie, 2017). In this section, we describe the South African achievement using IRT mean scores for the different content areas tested, and present the Rasch analyses to describe what South African learners know and can do at different points on the achievement scale.

13.1 International science curriculum analysis

The TIMSS curriculum and assessment framework is organised around the science content domains of biology, chemistry, physics and earth science. The TIMSS 2015 achievement instruments included trend and new items[16]. Table 13.1 presents the match between the TIMSS and South African curriculum in terms of content and cognitive domains.

---

[15] See Table 3.1 for the descriptors.
[16] See Methodology section in the Appendix for further details.

Table 13.1: Match between TIMSS and South African curriculum and achievement scores by content and cognitive domains [17], 2015

	% score points of assessment	Degree of science topic match between TIMSS and SA curriculum[18]	Degree of science item match between TIMSS and CAPS[19]	Scaled score mean (SE)	Difference from South African overall mean
Overall science score	100	91	81	358 (5.6)	
Content domains	100				
Biology	36	100	71	356 (5.9)	-2
Chemistry	19	67	96	369 (6.1)	+11
Physics	24	100	82	359 (5.5)	+1
Earth science	21	100	90	330 (6.4)	-28
Cognitive domains	100				
Knowing	36			337 (6.7)	-21
Applying	41			368 (5.9)	+10
Reasoning	23			350 (5.6)	-8

The TIMSS Curriculum Questionnaire listed the topics to be assessed in the TIMSS achievement instruments. South African curriculum experts linked the TIMSS topic areas to the South African curriculum. The science topics areas assessed in TIMSS 2015 and the South African curriculum are a 91 per cent match. We extended the analyses to the item level and each achievement item was examined for its fit to the South African curriculum. The match of specific science items assessed in TIMSS 2015 and the South African curriculum is 81 per cent.

Learner performance in the biology and physics content areas is close to the South African overall mean, while the mean score for chemistry is 11 points higher and for earth science 28 points lower than the overall mean score[20].

The TIMSS items are categorised into the following cognitive domains: 36 per cent knowledge, 41 per cent applying and 23 per cent reasoning. Knowledge items are the least difficult and reasoning items are the most difficult. The average performance for knowledge and reasoning items is lower than the overall South African science performance (by 21 points and 8 points respectively) and South African learners, surprisingly, performed higher for application items (by 10 points) than the overall mean score.

The international perspective is an important way to assess how South African learners are doing relative to their international peers. In this report, we go a step further in exploring the TIMSS data for South Africa by developing national proficiency benchmarks.

13.2 National science curriculum analysis

The difference between an international and national perspective is that the international benchmarks were based on the TIMSS international framework of what learners in all participating countries are expected to know, establishing trends over time. The national benchmarks focused on the performance of South African learners for TIMSS 2015 and attempts to unpack the knowledge and skills that learners are able to demonstrate at various points on the achievement continuum. The benchmarks were developed by a team of researchers in collaboration with the HSRC TIMSS team. Rasch analysis was used to construct a measure for both item difficulty and learner ability to correspond to an achievement scale of 0 – 1 000. Rasch works by using a mathematical model for predicting the probability of success of a learner on each test item. The Rasch model is a one-parameter model that

---

[17] The descriptions of the content and cognitive domains are found in the Description of the TIMSS Methodology in the Appendix section.
[18] The degree of match calculated as a proportion of topics (for each content area) covered by the Grade 8/9 South African curriculum. There is a total of 18 broad topics: six in biology; three in chemistry, five in physics and four in earth science. This information appeared in the TIMSS Curriculum Questionnaire.
[19] This refers to a National Curriculum Analysis using the DBE 2011 CAPS.
[20] The earth science topic areas are covered in the social science (geography) curriculum.

PART F

Science curriculum insights from national and international benchmarks

focuses on difficulty and rests on the assumption that all items have the same discrimination power but differ in terms of difficulty (Traub & Wolfe, 1981). The Rasch model uses the parameter item difficulty, where item difficulty is defined as the position on a latent trait variable in which a person has a 50 per cent probability of a correct response (McCamey, 2002). The more the participant's ability exceeds the item difficulty, the more likely it is that a person will answer the item correctly. The Rasch model transforms measures into interval measures, constructed by means of a stochastic process that creates inferential stability and locates the item difficulty and person ability on the latent continuum (Bond & Fox, 2015).

A Rasch score was generated for each learner that participated in TIMSS 2015. Table 13.2 shows the benchmarks and performance level descriptors that were derived from analysing the performance of South African learners in the TIMSS science assessment. The analysis of the national sample proposed seven distinct proficiency benchmarks, at particular Rasch score cut-off points, for Grade 9 learners in South Africa. These ranged from 'far below basic' for the lowest performers to 'advanced' for the top achievers. Learners in benchmark 3 were at a 'basic' level of proficiency. Learners in benchmark 6 were 'highly proficient' in Grade 9 science based on the local achievement distribution and curriculum requirements (details in the working paper).

Table 13.2: Proficiency level descriptors for the South African benchmark exercise, 2015

Benchmark	Rasch[21] Scale units	Proficiency description
1	<400	**Far below basic:** Very low performance where learners have very little understanding of the knowledge and skills in the TIMSS science assessment
2	400 to 449.99	**Below basic:** Low performance where learners demonstrate rudimentary knowledge and skills included in the TIMSS science assessment
3	450 to 499.99	**Basic:** Limited performance where learners demonstrate a partial understanding of the knowledge and skills included in the TIMSS science assessment
4	500 to 549.99	**Just proficient:** Satisfactory performance where learners demonstrate sufficient knowledge and skills included in the TIMSS science assessment
5	550 to 599.99	**Average proficient:** Solid performance where learners demonstrate competent knowledge and skills included in the TIMSS science assessment
6	600 to 649.99	**Highly proficient:** Far above average performance where learners demonstrate broad knowledge and skills included in the TIMSS science assessment
7	>650	**Advanced:** Superior performance where learners demonstrate a comprehensive and complex understanding of the knowledge and skills included in the TIMSS science assessment

An advantage of the Rasch measurement is that meaning can be attached to learner scores. That is, we can determine what learners can actually do if they obtain a particular TIMSS score. This is a powerful tool because substantive meanings can be given to scores in terms of the skills or proficiencies in mathematics and science. A science item map which linked TIMSS items to particular Rasch scores was generated.

13.3 Developing national benchmarks and proficiency label descriptors

A crucial step in the methodology involved consulting South African science curriculum experts. They evaluated the items at each level and identified the skills required and the content covered at each of the benchmarks. Here we use the science results to demonstrate the value of this approach for policy makers and practitioners.

Curriculum specialists reviewed each of the 259 science items, under secure conditions, on the TIMSS science test to evaluate whether the concepts belonged to the following areas of the CAPS curriculum: Grade 4 to 6 natural sciences, Grade 7 to 9 natural sciences, or Grade 7 to 9 earth sciences. Items related to life sciences were reviewed based on the following section of the CAPS curriculum: CAPS curriculum of CAPS Life Skills Gr R-3, CAPS Natural Sciences and Technology Gr 4 to 9, or CAPS Social Sciences for Gr 7 to 9. They also highlighted items whose content was beyond the Grade 9 curriculum and was based on content covered in the South African FET Grades 10 to 12 curriculum. Also noted were items that were not part of any of these strands.

---

[21] The Rasch scale is not equivalent to the IRT scale units used in the earlier parts of the report.

Test items were grouped into four cognitive domains based on the language used in CAPS. These were: knowledge, comprehension, application and logical questions. For *knowledge* items, learners had to recall facts. In theory, they could do so without a thorough understanding of the related concepts. *Comprehension* items required learners to use their knowledge in examples that they might not have encountered, to explain a concept through an example or to identify concepts that were applicable to a question among others in a list. *Application* items required learners to interpret situations and predict outcomes based on concepts that they had learned and understood. This was a higher order thinking skill and overlapped to a certain extent with logical reasoning. The *logical* reasoning category included critical reasoning and integration of knowledge. Learners needed to analyse the context of the question, decide which concepts were applicable and reason logically about the information provided.

All TIMSS science items were then categorised to the proficiency benchmarks and cognitive domains (Table 13.3).

Table 13.3: Cognitive categories per proficiency benchmark for all science content areas, 2015

	Knowledge	Compre-hension	Application	Logical reasoning	Not classified in the four categories *	Not in CAPS **	Total
Benchmark 1	4	5	1	1	0	0	11
Benchmark 2	13	16	17	9	4	6	59
Benchmark 3	17	17	14	11	7	14	66
Benchmark 4	14	19	15	16	8	17	72
Benchmark 5	6	10	7	7	6	11	36
Benchmark 6 and 7	2	0	3	8	2	5	15
Total	56	67	57	52	27	53	259

* They could not be classified in any of the four categories since they are considered to be too difficult and falls outside the scope of the average Grade 9 learner.
** The items indicated in the column are among the items that fall outside the Grades 4-6 or Grades 7-9 curriculum.

Source: (Scherman et al., 2017). Note that the numbers shown in the table are the authors' calculations.

The observations from the analysis of the TIMSS items that could affect the achievement are as follows:

- There are some items in the assessment that are not linked to the CAPS Grades 4 to 9 curricula, and this accounts for 19 per cent of all items. One-third of these items relate to knowledge in the Grades 10 to 12 curriculum. Some of these items may be classified as general knowledge, but if a learner has not been exposed to this knowledge before, they may not be able to answer correctly.

- Given that only one-third of the learners spoke the language of the test at home, the language used in constructing an item could be a factor that complicates the way that learners respond to test items. In addition, learners may not be familiar with the scientific language (e.g. corrode, oxidation, Cartesian, permafrost, monarch butterflies, deer mice, manx cats) required to understand an item.

- Some science items require using mathematical concepts to answer the questions and learners do not make the link with the mathematical knowledge domains.

- South African learners seem to be struggling with questions classified as knowledge items. It is disconcerting that many knowledge items fell into higher performance benchmarks 4, 5 and 6.

Using the categorisation of items at the different benchmark levels, the curriculum specialists further described each item in the band in terms of the content and cognitive skill required. This then gives us a sense what learners could do at each performance level for science and what they would need to learn to move to the next proficiency level (Table 13.4).

PART F

Science curriculum insights from national and international benchmarks

Table 13.4: Science proficiency descriptions, 2015

Rasch achievement range	Proficiency level description	What learners can do
Benchmark 1 <400	Far below basic	Learners have basic knowledge of atoms and compounds, properties of metals and materials
Benchmark 2 400 to 449.99	Below basic	Learners have a basic knowledge of chemical reactions, visible light, potential and kinetic energy, electromagnets, plate tectonics, recycling Learners comprehend concepts motion, forces and levers, the atmosphere, mimicry and migration Learners can recall information related to the digestive system, photosynthesis, energy flow, cells as the basic unit of life Learners demonstrate that they can read graphs
Benchmark 3 450 to 499.99	Basic	Learners can describe and recognise elements, compounds, mixtures, non-metals as insulators, thermal equilibrium Learners can explain speed of sound in different mediums, parallel circuits, solution concentrations Learners can interpret information related to the sun and the earth, physical changes, pressure in a fluid, electrical cells Learners have knowledge and comprehension of diseases, plant and animal cells, adaptations to the environment, tissues, support systems in animals and animal skeletons
Benchmark 4 500 to 549.99	Just proficient	Learners have knowledge of reflection of light, pH, change of states Learners can apply knowledge related to astronomy, chemical formulae, atoms and particle model of matter, electric conductors and insulators, magnets, resultant of horizontal forces, adaptation and population ecology Learners can interpret information related to the cell as the basic unit of life, microorganisms, respiration, circulatory systems and nutrition, elements, compounds, mixtures, use V=IR for calculation
Benchmark 5 550 to 599.99	Average proficient	Learners can use knowledge related to forces, acids and bases, gravitational forces Learners can apply information related to the solar system, particle model of matter, heat transfer, rate of dissolving, mechanical energy, speed of light and sound, water cycle, rock cycle, life cycles, respiration, interactions and interdependence within the environment, genetics and biodiversity
Benchmark 6 600 to 649.99	Highly proficient	Learners apply knowledge related to heat transfer, properties of solids, liquids and gases, chemical reactions, the earth and the moon, pressure as force per unit area and the particle model of matter
Benchmark 7 >650	Advanced	Learners can explain and apply information related to pressure as force per unit area, density and volume Learners can evaluate information related to climate, evolution, population dynamics and reproduction in plants

Section summary

The TIMSS achievement instrument is designed to respond to the curricula of 39 countries. There is a high level of overlap with the South African CAPS curriculum with 91 per cent topic overlap and 81 per cent item overlap. The earth science curriculum is covered in the social sciences subject, and not in the natural sciences and technology curriculum. Compared to the overall average, performance is higher in the chemistry section and lower in the earth science section. Unlike their international counterparts, South African learners score far lower than the South African overall average in knowledge items. TIMSS uses IRT analyses to describe learner achievement. The South African data were analysed using a Rasch analysis and the descriptions of what learners can do in the different bands, could help curriculum planners in designing appropriate interventions.

PART **G**

KEY FINDINGS, POLICY IMPLICATIONS AND RECOMMENDATIONS

Key findings, policy implications and recommendations

This report presented the findings of the TIMSS 2015 Grade 9 study in South Africa. It was also written to provide some perspective about how the results of international assessments can be used to provide meaningful national insights. The section that follows brings together the main findings from the descriptive, inferential and psychometric analyses and provides some policy recommendations for improving educational quality.

1. *The value in participating in international assessments is increased when the results are used for understanding national conditions.* South Africa's participation in TIMSS over the last twenty years has enriched our understanding of learner performance and how the country is ranked relative to other education systems around the world. Raising performance standards can improve a country's economic competitiveness. Therefore, the global perspective is an important one. South Africa's membership in the TIMSS community has also helped to develop the capacity of local researchers and increased the technical rigour of our large-scale assessments. The global perspective was supplemented by a national one. The South African analysis included the identification of a group of potential learners. These are learners who are close to the minimum competency benchmarks as defined by TIMSS. Additional Rasch analysis of the South African results can better inform policy makers about what mathematics and science skills Grade 9 learners have acquired.

2. *South African mathematics and science achievement scores have improved from a 'very low' (1995, 1999, 2003) to a 'low' (2011, 2015) national average.* South Africa is still one of the lower-performing countries in mathematics and science in comparison to other TIMSS participating countries. However, from 2003 to 2015 the country has shown the biggest positive improvement of all participating countries in both mathematics (by 90 points) and science (by 87 points), which is equivalent to an improvement in achievement by two grade levels. Average performance in the public school system and among historically weaker provinces has clearly improved but most Grade 9 learners are yet to achieve a minimum level of competency in mathematics and science, based on the TIMSS international perspective.

3. *South African achievement continues to remain highly unequal but there has been a slight decline in inequality between schools over time.* Like other low-performing countries, only one-third of South African learners achieved a mathematics and science score above the benchmark of 400 points, a score denoting the minimum level of competence. When the achievement scores are broken down by school type, the patterns reveal vast inequalities. Approximately 80 per cent of learners attending independent schools, 60 per cent of learners at fee-paying and 20 per cent of learners at no-fee schools achieved mathematics scores above the minimum level of competency. Within this unequal performance, it is also worth noting that 3.2 per cent of South African mathematics learners and 4.9 per cent of science learners achieved mathematics and science scores at the *high* level of achievement (above 550 points).

4. *Almost half the Grade 9 learners in the school system are over-age.* The pattern is different based on school types with 43 per cent of learners in no-fee schools, 64 per cent in fee-paying and 73 per cent in independent schools at the appropriate age. The achievement scores of over-age learners is much lower than age-grade appropriate learners, suggesting that simply spending an extra year in a grade is not leading to more learning. For grade repetition to lead to improved learning outcomes, repeat learners must receive extra learning support. This must start at the foundation phase otherwise the performance levels will widen as learners progress through the education system.

5. *The importance of LoLT for mathematics and science goes further than previously considered in TIMSS. The influence of language was evident throughout this study.* The national benchmarking exercise emphasised that language skills were important for answering any item on the test regardless of the level of difficulty. At home, parents who were not fluent in the language of instruction struggled to provide homework support for their children. At school, less fluency in the language of the test (either English or Afrikaans) was related to lower test scores. Learners who spoke the language of the test more frequently, achieved better results and this was over and above the effect of SES. This implies that all learners, regardless of their SES, are disadvantaged by lack of language fluency. Moreover, fluency in the LoLT does not guarantee academic success. The language of mathematics and science in the classroom may present a completely different set of challenges if words that learners are familiar with take on a different meaning in the classroom context. Addressing the role of language is not easy nor is it quick. The goal is not to make learners more capable in the use of language simply for testing purposes, but to ensure that they are better equipped to understand the nuances of the materials covered in mathematics and science.

6. *Resources matter but educational success goes beyond improving resource access.* Learners from no-fee schools had the most limited access to home resources, although there has been some improvement in terms of equalising home access to running tap water, water-flush toilets and electricity. Access to technology remained exclusive to wealthier learners. The evidence on school resources was both heartening and disappointing. It was encouraging that physical resources had an independent and positive association with average school achievement. This means that policies that have worked to improve access to school resources can continue to play a positive role in improving educational quality. However, narrowing the achievement gap between no-fee, fee-paying and independent schools is not as simple as just improving resource access. Forty per cent of learners in fee-paying schools and 20 per cent of learners in independent schools failed to meet the minimum level of competency set by TIMSS. Maintaining the momentum around resource accessibility and efficient utility must continue but this is only part of the solution for improving performance and equity between schools. Human resource challenges were greater in public schools and it was more difficult to fill vacancies in these environments. Strategies to recruit and retain the best subject-specific teaching professionals into public schools needs to continue.

7. *The climate of the school counts.* Schools with a healthier school climate (emphasis on academic success, safety and order, fewer disciplinary problems, fewer incidences of bullying and fewer challenges faced by teachers) had higher average achievement scores. A significant part of the achievement gaps between no-fee, fee-paying and independent schools was explained by the type of climate in the school. Also worth noting was that many different dimensions of school climate made a difference. In as much as improving school climate needs to be prioritised, a broad view needs to be adopted when studying the climate of the school. The goal should be to understand how the organisational and professional conditions of the school can support learning. Because the climate of the school will reflect the climate of the community in which it is based, a healthy school climate requires the input and support of school management and the community at large.

PART G

Key findings, policy implications and recommendations

8. *Greater expectations endure in spite of the academic difficulties faced by many learners.* Some learners from no-fee schools did not plan to further their education beyond secondary school; and yet there was a high percentage of learners with a low socioeconomic profile who aspired to obtaining an advanced degree. Learners from public schools were also more likely to attend extra lessons, either to excel in class or keep up in class. Further research is needed to understand how extra lessons fit into teaching and learning. It is unclear whether learners attended extra lessons by choice, whether these lessons were paid for or offered as a service by the community. Because learner support programmes may take many different forms, it is crucial that their quality be regulated and that, wherever possible, learners receive support from accredited organisations. Some would suggest that ambitions for further study are unrealistic, given the many hurdles that these learners will face just to complete secondary school. We take a different view. We would like to think that an enduring faith in the transformative power of education remains. It is the responsibility of educational leaders to ensure that these hopes are fulfilled.

9. *Continued analyses using local benchmarks should be encouraged to inform curriculum reform more effectively.* We identified 35 per cent of mathematics learners and 28 per cent of science learners in the group of potential learners (scoring between 325 and 400 TIMSS points). With a greater investment, especially in no-fee schools, this group could improve their scores to over 400. The Rasch analysis created national proficiency benchmarks based on South Africa's learner performance. This provided a better sense of the specific competency levels that exist in South Africa and what learners knew relative to the local curriculum requirements. Most importantly, this process revealed in practical terms what teachers needed to cover to help learners move from one benchmark to another. Policy makers, researchers and practitioners would do well to build on this exercise so that local and international assessments can be better integrated. This is not an easy undertaking, but building the links between local and international studies is crucial for future monitoring purposes.

Policy recommendations for different role players

National	• Continue to use international assessments to track progress towards education targets. Develop systems that enable the results of national and international assessments to be compared
	• Strengthen meaningful language development in home language and LoLT
	• Develop a set of specific targets for fee-paying and no-fee schools
	• Prioritise the provisioning of pedagogical infrastructure (e.g. libraries and laboratories) and pedagogical resources (e.g. workbooks and textbooks) to learners in public schools, especially no-fee schools
	• Continue to update the National School Safety Framework to include additional aspects of school climate
	• Develop accountability systems to ensure the competence of newly appointed school principals
	• Create incentives for teachers to work at schools where there are acute shortages
Provincial	• Ensure that pedagogical infrastructure and resources (especially textbooks) are in schools and used effectively
	• Promote awareness about the importance of a healthy school climate
	• Maintain efforts to recruit and retain subject-specific teaching professionals in public schools
	• Continue to monitor the implementation of the National School Safety Framework for public schools
District	• Design appropriate interventions for improving the use of language in teaching mathematics and science
	• Monitor teacher and learner attendance and punctuality
	• Monitor the availability of LTSM (especially textbooks) and evaluate how effectively these materials are used
	• Share best practices for developing teacher capacity through communities of practice
	• Monitor violations of school safety and support schools in improving school climate
School	• Ensure safety, discipline and order
	• Monitor and manage rates of absenteeism among teachers and learners
	• Promote an academic culture in schools
	• Develop additional programmes for learners who are repeating a grade
Teachers and classrooms	• Encourage reading and writing in African languages
	• Emphasise punctuality among teachers
	• Evaluate and improve on teacher subject matter knowledge and pedagogy
	• Provide learners with practice examples and regular feedback
Learners	• Increase reading and writing activities
	• Emphasise punctuality and attendance among learners
	• Improve proficiency in the language of the test
	• Regular practice of mathematics and science examples with written homework
Communities	• Motivate and mentor young children about the importance of education
	• Decrease levels of violence in the community
	• Support school efforts to improve the school climate
	• Monitor teacher and learner attendance at schools
Households	• Support and monitor homework and school reports
	• Monitor learner attendance and punctuality at schools
	• Instil a culture of zero tolerance of violence
	• Engage with teachers and school officials about education delivery, school climate, learner support programmes and performance

PART G

EDUCATION

KNOWLEDGE TRAINING TEACHER THEORY TEST INFORMATION

APPENDIX

APPENDIX A:
Summary of results: TIMSS 2015

Table A1 provides the summary results of average mathematics and science achievement scores as well as home and school resources by school type.

Table A1: Summary of results, TIMSS Grade 9 2015

	No fee schools	Fee paying schools	Independent schools
Learner achievement	341 (3.3)	423 (10.0)	477 (11.5)
Average mathematics score (SE)	317 (4.2)	425 (11.9)	485 (11.8)
Average science score (SE)			
% of learners achieving at or above 400 in mathematics (SE)	19.0 (1.9)	59.6 (9.7)	80.6 (16.7)
% of learners achieving at or above 400 in science (SE)	16.4 (1.8)	58.5 (9.3)	81.0 (15.9)
Age			
Average age of learners in years	15.9	15.4	15.2
Home resources			
% of learners with basic home resources:			
Electricity	87.0	96.0	98.0
Running tap water	64.0	91.0	95.0
Water-flush toilets	44.0	90.0	94.0
% of learners with pedagogical resources:			
Computer	22.0	45.0	72.0
Internet connection	45.0	71.0	84.0
No or few books at home	46.0	37.0	26.0
% of learners with more educated parents			
Maternal education above Grade 12	64.0	84.0	92.0
Parent with university education	15.5	31.4	48.2
Language			
% of learners who always or almost always spoke the test language at home	19.3	51.1	56.9
School physical resources			
% of learners not affected by resource shortage			
Mathematics	1.6	9.0	59.0
Science	2.2	9.3	59.0
% of learners whose teachers use textbooks as basis of instruction			
Mathematics	79.8	59.8	56.1
Science	68.1	57.7	61.0
% of learners whose teachers use workbooks as basis of instruction			
Mathematics	53.3	35.4	39.5
Science	36.4	39.6	31.4
School environment and climate			
Teachers arriving late: not a problem	32.6	44.2	72.3
Teachers absenteeism: not a problem	23.0	30.4	68.5
Learners arriving late: not a problem	10.3	6.7	22.3
Learners absenteeism: not a problem	7.7	2.1	44.4
School safety			
% of learners affected by school discipline and safety: moderate problem	39.3	6.5	2.7
% of learners who have almost never experienced bullying	30.8	45.4	54.0

APPENDIX B:
TIMSS 2015 design and methodology

1. Introduction

TIMSS 2015 was the sixth cycle of the IEA series of large-scale assessments of learner achievement dedicated to improving teaching and learning in mathematics and science. More than 39 very diverse countries participated in TIMSS 2015 at the Grade 8 or 9 levels; where diversities ranged from economic development, geographic location to population size.

Drawing on the TIMSS 2015 Assessment Framework[22] we will explain the design and implementation of the study. The main stages in the design and planning for TIMSS are:

- TIMSS conceptual framework
- Instruments to measure achievement and learning context
- Sampling
- Field testing
- Main administration
- Scoring of constructed responses
- Data capture and cleaning
- Reporting TIMSS achievement scores

2. TIMSS conceptual framework

TIMSS uses the curriculum as the major organising concept in considering how educational opportunities are provided to learners and the factors that affect how learners use these opportunities. The TIMSS Curriculum Model has three aspects: the intended curriculum, the implemented curriculum, and the attained curriculum (Figure 1). These represent the mathematics and science that learners are expected to learn as defined by countries' curricular policies and publications, how the educational system should be organised to facilitate this learning, what is actually taught in classrooms, the characteristics of those teaching it, how it is taught, and, finally, what it is that learner have learned.

Figure B1: TIMSS Curriculum Model

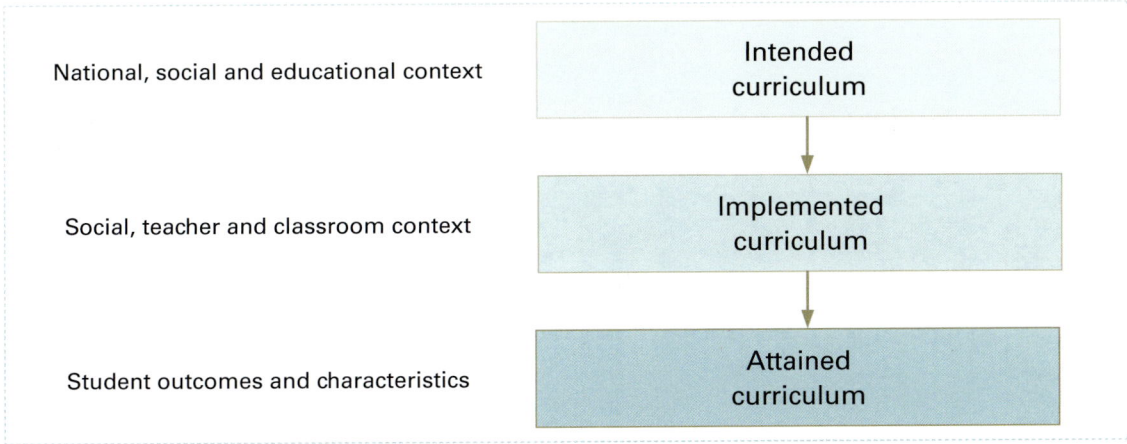

The three content domains are assessed for both mathematics and science and are described in Table B1. The percentage of the assessment that is covered by each content domain is also shown.

---

[22] Mullis IVS & Martin MO (Eds.) (2013). TIMSS 2015 Assessment Frameworks. Retrieved from Boston College, TIMSS & PIRLS International Study Center website: http://timssandpirls.bc.edu/timss2015/frameworks.html

APPENDIX

APPENDIX B:
TIMSS 2015 design and methodology

Table B1: TIMSS Grade 9 content domains for mathematics and science

Mathematics				
Content domain	Number	Algebra	Geometry	Data and probability
% of assessment	30	30	20	20
Topics	Integers Fractions and decimals Ratio, proportion, and per cent	Expressions, operations, and equations Relationships and functions	Geometric shapes and measurements	Data probability
Science				
Content domain	Biology	Chemistry	Physics	Earth science
% of assessment	35	20	25	20
Topics	Characteristics and life processes of organisms Cells and their functions Life cycles, reproduction, and heredity Diversity, adaptation, and natural selection Ecosystems Human health	Composition of matter Properties of matter Chemical change	Physical states and changes in matter Energy transformation and transfer Light and sound Electricity and magnetism Motion and forces	Earth's structure and physical features Earth's processes, cycles, and history Earth's resources, their use, and conservation Earth in the solar system and the universe

In order for learners to correctly complete the TIMSS assessment items they need to draw on a range of cognitive skills. These skills are addressed in terms of three cognitive domains set out in Table B2.

Table B2: TIMSS Grade 9 cognitive domains for mathematics and science

	Mathematics (% of assessment)	Mathematics skills assessed	Science (% of assessment)	Science skills assessed
Knowing	35	Recall Recognise Classify Compute Retrieve Measure	35	Recall/recognise Describe Provide examples
Applying	40	Determine Represent Model Implement	35	Compare Relate Use models Interpret information Explain
Reasoning	25	Analyse Integrate Synthesise Draw conclusions Generalise Justify	30	Analyse Synthesise Hypothesise Evaluate Draw conclusions Generalise Justify

3. Instruments measuring learner achievement and context

A set of research instruments pertaining to learner achievement items and background information is developed by the IEA with input from the various countries participating in the study. These instruments will be discussed in the following sections.

3.1. Achievement booklets

The TIMSS Achievement Booklets contain trend items. Trend items are used to measure trends but also to rescale or calibrate items between cycles. After every cycle items are released and replaced with new items in the next cycle. The new items are generated in National Research Coordinator meetings and are subjected to extensive validation processes.

Throughout the TIMSS studies, vast numbers of items have accumulated and with every cycle certain items are released into the public domain. Those that are used as trend items are not released. By releasing items into the public domain, countries are able to use these items as examples for preparation for the next TIMSS cycle. The HSRC sent all the released items to the sampled schools on a CD and these items appear on the DBE's Thutong website.

In order to ensure maximum curriculum coverage, TIMSS uses a matrix sampling approach where items are arranged into blocks. The TIMSS items are spread across 14 booklets and a single booklet is administered to learners.

3.2. Background questionnaires

To obtain better insights and explanations for the achievement scores, TIMSS included a number of background questionnaires. Four questionnaires are administered in addition to the assessment instruments; these are:

- The **Learner background questionnaire** which is completed by the learner who completed the assessment and asks about aspects of the learners' home and school lives, their home environment, school climate for learning and their perceptions and attitudes towards mathematics and science.

- The **Teacher questionnaire** is administered to the mathematics and science teachers of the learners who wrote the assessment tests. The questionnaire was designed to gather information on teacher characteristics as well as classroom contexts for teaching and learning mathematics and science.

- The **School questionnaire** is administered to the principal in all sampled schools. It asks about school characteristics like instructional time, resources and technology as well as parental involvement.

- The **Curriculum questionnaire** is completed by the National Research Coordinator who is required to complete information pertaining to the curriculum which is followed by South African public schools.

4. Sampling

A sample of Grade 9 schools was selected to provide a national estimate of mathematics and science scores. TIMSS 2015 followed the sampling procedures as prescribed in the TIMSS methods and procedures manual[23]. TIMSS follows a two-stage stratified cluster sampling design; where 300 schools were selected with probability proportionate to size at the first stage and at the second stage an intact Grade 9 class was selected within each of the sampled schools.

APPENDIX

[23] Martin MO, Mullis IVS & Hooper M (Eds.). (2016). Methods and Procedures in TIMSS 2015. Retrieved from Boston College, TIMSS & PIRLS International Study Center website: http://timssandpirls.bc.edu/publications/timss/2015-methods.html

APPENDIX B:
TIMSS 2015 design and methodology

At stage 1 a representative sample of schools was drawn using the DBE's master list of schools for 2013 as the sampling frame. Schools included in the sampling frame were schools that offered Grade 9 classes and had no missing information on the stratification variables. The sample was explicitly stratified by province, type of school (public and independent schools) and LoLT (English, Afrikaans and dual medium).

Stage 2 involved sampling classes. For classes to be sampled within schools, schools were required to submit class information for all Grade 9 classes. An intact class was randomly selected using sampling software provided by the IEA Data Processing Centre (DPC) called Windows-School Sampling Software (WinW3S). Generally, one class per school was randomly selected. However, in dual medium schools, two classes were selected. In addition to the sample of participating schools, a first and second replacement school were selected in the event that a school was unable to participate.

Table B3: Schools and learners, by province, participating in TIMSS 2015

	Schools sampled	Schools sample participated	First replacement	Second replacement	Total schools	Total learners
EC	36	33	1		34	1 523
FS	30	29			29	1 142
GT	47	41	3	2	46	1 654
KZ	34	31	1		32	1 326
LP	36	35	2		37	1 782
MP	28	28	1		29	1 391
NC	29	29			29	1 261
NW	29	26			26	1 010
WC	31	30			30	1 425
Grand total	300	282	8	2	292	12 514

The TIMSS 2015 realised sample included 292 principals, 331 science teachers, 334 mathematics teachers and 12 514 learners.

5. Field testing

Pilot studies or field tests in TIMSS are done for a number of reasons, namely:

• To serve as a dress rehearsal for the main survey;

• To provide important information about how well items are functioning; and

• To measure the validity and reliability of the various questionnaire scales/indices.

The sample for the field test was drawn simultaneously with the sample of the main survey; using the same sampling procedures as for the main study. The sample size for the field test was 15 schools (five per cent of the main sample total) with a target of 600 learners. The sample design ensured that a school drawn for the field test was not selected again for the main survey. The pilot was administered in Gauteng and KwaZulu-Natal. These schools were within a 100-kilometre radius of the Pretoria city centre in the case of Gauteng and Durban in the case of KwaZulu-Natal.

6.   Main administration

There was a large amount of preparatory work done before the study was administered. The international TIMSS team provided countries with very strict guidelines on how the preparation needed to be done. All these procedures can be found, and described in detail, in the TIMSS 2015 survey operations procedures (unit 1 to 7) documents within the TIMSS 2015 Methods and Procedures report[24].

Pre-administration contact with schools is extremely important as it allowed the HSRC to obtain permission to conduct the study, to access class lists with learner information as well as to arrange appointments with the schools to administer the study.

Consistency between countries is important and the international team developed two basic procedures to guide countries through the data collection phase:

6.1   Administration of the main survey

The main survey was administered by an external fieldwork company with relevant qualifications and experience in the field of educational assessment. South Africa administered the main study in the last two weeks of August into the first week of September 2015. The HSRC worked with the DBE and provincial coordinators to ensure that the study was successfully administered.

6.2   Monitoring the quality of the survey administration

Quality assurance of the fieldwork is important as it allows for valid learner achievement comparisons between and within countries. Ten per cent of the sampled schools were randomly selected and senior HSRC researchers served as National Quality Control Monitors to monitor the TIMSS administration processes. In addition, the International TIMSS team selected and trained an International Quality Control Monitor. The International Quality Control Monitor monitored the administration processes in 29 schools in South Africa.

7.   Scoring the constructed response items

The constructed response (open-ended) items represent approximately 50 per cent of the TIMSS assessments, hence the reliability and validity of scoring is critical to the quality of the assessment results. In order to achieve reliable and valid scoring, the IEA provided training, comprehensive scoring guides and scoring procedures. Learners' responses were scored consistently, regardless of who is assigning the scores. The HSRC employed teachers and university students to conduct the scoring. As a quality control measure, five per cent of the booklets were marked twice by different scorers to check for consistency. This is referred to as reliability scoring. Moderating of scoring quality was done by the HSRC staff on an ongoing basis for maintaining accurate and consistent scoring throughout the process.

8.   Data capture and cleaning

All data was captured using a software program developed by the IEA called Data Management Expert (DME). The HSRC double captured all data and verified against the original capture. This ensured that the data remained below the acceptable error rate of 0.1 per cent for assessment data and one per cent for contextual data. Once all validation steps were performed on the data, it was sent to the IEA DPC in Germany for the final phase of cleaning. The IEA remained in contact with data managers at the HSRC during the cleaning process.

APPENDIX

---

[24] *Martin, MO, Mullis IVS & Hooper M (Eds.). (2016). Methods and Procedures in TIMSS 2015. Retrieved from Boston College, TIMSS & PIRLS International Study Center website: http://timssandpirls.bc.edu/publications/timss/2015-methods.html*

APPENDIX B:
TIMSS 2015 design and methodology

9. Reporting TIMSS achievement scores

Due to the TIMSS item block design, IRT scaling methods generated five plausible values to obtain estimated proficiency scores in mathematics and science. Each learner responded to about 70 items. Using statistical methods and demographic background for similar learners, a score was imputed for each learner. This design solicits relatively few responses from each sampled student while maintaining a wide range of content representation when responses are aggregated across all learners. With this approach, the advantage of estimating population characteristics is offset by the inability to make precise statements about individuals[25].

The TIMSS 2015 achievement results are summarised using IRT scaling and report mathematics achievement scores on a scale with a mean of 500 and a standard deviation of 100 together with a SE, which refers to the statistical accuracy of the estimate.

---

[25] TIMSS and PIRLS Achievement Scaling Methodology Retrieved from
https://timssandpirls.bc.edu/methods/pdf/TP11_Scaling_Methodology.pdf

APPENDIX C:
Summary of South Africa's mathematics curriculum

Mathematics curriculum
Grade R – 9 summarised

The summary represents the content of the South African mathematics curriculum based on the National Curriculum and Assessment Policy Statement (CAPS). CAPS provides guidelines for teaching and learning in South African schools.

	Content domains	Process application
		Foundation phase
Grade R	Numbers, operations and relationships	• Number concept development up to 10 • Describe, compare and order objects up to 10 • Solve problems in context up to 10 • Addition and subtraction up to 10
	Patterns, functions, and algebra	• Using colours and shapes
	Space and shape (Geometry)	• Recognise objects • Understand position and direction • Use 3D objects
	Measurement	• Compare and order length, height and weight
	Data handling	• Collect and organise objects
Grade 1	Numbers, operations and relationships	• Number concept development up to 20 • Describe, compare and order objects up to 20 • Solve problems in context up to 20 • Addition and subtraction up to 20
	Patterns, functions, and algebra	• Copying, extending and describing simple patterns and number sequence
	Space and shape (Geometry)	• Recognising and naming 2D and 3D objects in the classroom and in pictures
	Measurement	• Talking about the passing of time • Telling the time • Informal measuring
	Data handling	• Collecting and organising objects • Answering questions about data in pictograph
Grade 2	Numbers, operations and relationships	• Revising Grade 1 work by including numbers up to 200 • Ordering and recognising objects up to 99 • Recognising the place value of two-digit numbers to 99 • Solving problems and explaining solutions to problems with answers up to 50 • Recognising and identifying the South African bank notes up to R50
	Patterns, functions, and algebra	• Using and naming unitary fractions including halves, quarters, thirds and fifths • Creating and describing own patterns in geometry
	Space and shape (Geometry)	• Recognising and naming 3D objects i.e. cylinders
	Measurement	• Using calendars and clocks to calculate and describe lengths of time • Introducing formal measuring of capacity and volume
	Data handling	• Collect and organise data; represent data in pictograph • Analyse and interpret data

APPENDIX C:
Summary of South Africa's mathematics curriculum

	Content domains	Process application
Grade 3	Numbers, operations and relationships	• Revising Grade 2 work by including numbers up to 1 000 • Ordering and recognising objects up to 999 • Recognising the place value of two-digit numbers to 999 • Solving word problems in context and explaining own solution to problems involving addition and subtraction with answers up to 999 • Converting between Rands and cents
	Patterns, functions, and algebra	• Copy, extend and describe patterns
	Space and shape (Geometry)	• Recognising and naming 3D objects • Using and naming unitary fractions including halves, quarters, thirds and fifths
	Measurement	• Determining line of symmetry through paper folding and reflection
	Data handling	• Organising data in lists, tally marks and tables • Using bar graphs to interpret data
Intermediate phase		
Grade 4	Numbers, operations and relationships	• Mental calculation of whole numbers in units of 10 and 100, understanding expressions and relationships • Number range for counting, ordering, comparing and representing up to 1 000 • Solve problems in financial and measurement context • Addition, subtraction and division
	Patterns, functions, and algebra	• Investigate and extend patterns • Describe relationships in tables, flow diagram, verbally, and number sentence
	Space and shape (Geometry)	• Recognise, visualise, describe, compare and name properties of 2D and 3D shapes
	Measurement	• Describe symmetry • Practical measuring • Reading time
	Data handling	• Reading, interpreting and representing
Grade 5	Numbers, operations and relationships	• Evaluate, order, and compare 6-digit numbers • Solve problems in contexts involving common fractions, including grouping and sharing • Addition of 5-digit numbers, multiplication of 3- by 2-digit numbers, and division of 3- by 2-digit numbers
	Patterns, functions, and algebra	• Describe angles in shapes • Differentiate between squares and rectangles
	Space and shape (Geometry)	• Using practicals to understand the concept of shapes • Using transformations to make composite shapes and tessellations
	Measurement	• Exposure to stopwatches as an instrument to read time and thermometers to measure temperature
	Data handling	• Ranging data in ascending and descending order • Analysing the mode of data and compare frequencies

	Content domains	Process application
Grade 6	Numbers, operations and relationships	• 12- by 12-digit multiplication • Ordering 9-digit numbers; recognising, ordering, and calculating decimal fractions • Grouping and equal sharing with remainders • Finding percentages of whole numbers and using decimal points
	Patterns, functions, and algebra	• Representing numeric and geometric patterns on tables and describing general rules of the observed relationships
	Space and shape (Geometry)	• Understanding similarities and differences of rectangles and parallelograms, and the sizes of angles in 2D and 3D shapes • Using a pair of compasses to draw circles; making 3D models with straws and toothpicks
	Measurement	• Learning positions and movements on maps, reading time zones on maps, and calculating time differences based on time zones
	Data handling	• Evaluating questionnaires used to collect data, and analysing the mode and medium of data
	**Senior phase**	
Grade 7	Numbers, operations and relationships	• Listing prime factors and finding the LCM and HCF of numbers • Properties of integers, comparing and calculating integers • Ordering and comparing decimal fractions • Calculating and comparing numbers in exponential form
	Patterns, functions, and algebra	• Investigating numeric and geometric patterns by representing them in physical or diagram form • Determining formulae of functions; introduction of number sentences using algebraic expressions and algebraic language
	Space and shape (Geometry)	• Defining various straight lines • Transformation geometry with enlargements and reductions; measuring angles using a protractor • Analysing area, volume, and perimeter of 2D and 3D models
	Measurement	• Conversion of SI units • Use formula to calculate area and volume
	Data handling	• Grouping data into intervals • Representing data on graphs • Determining probabilities of outcomes
Grade 8	Numbers, operations and relationships	• Calculating square roots and cubic roots • Multiplying and dividing with integers • Recognising and using additive and multiplicative inverses for integers
	Patterns, functions, and algebra	• Understanding and solving algebraic expressions
	Space and shape (Geometry)	• Analysing extended features of graphs i.e. maximum and minimum, discrete and continuous • Plot graphs using points from table
	Measurement	• Investigating properties of geometric figures • Calculation of surface area and volume of triangular prisms • Developing and using the Theorem of Pythagoras
	Data handling	• Using questionnaires to collect data; analysing dispersion, error and biasness of data

APPENDIX

APPENDIX C:
Summary of South Africa's mathematics curriculum

	Content domains	Process application
Grade 9	Numbers, operations and relationships	• Solving problems in context involving ratio and rate, and direct and indirect proportions
	Patterns, functions, and algebra	• Factorising algebraic expressions; interpreting linear graphs i.e. x and y intercepts and gradients • Determining equations and drawing of linear graphs
	Space and shape (Geometry)	• Solving problems related to similar and congruent triangles • Recognising and describing properties of spheres and cylinders • Translation within and across quadrants in transformation geometry
	Measurement	• Exploring the sum of the interior angles of polygons • Solving problems using the Theorem of Pythagoras
	Data handling	• Identifying outliers in data using scatter plots to represent data • Comparing relative frequency with probability

APPENDIX D:
Summary of South Africa's science curriculum

Science curriculum
Grade R – 9 summarised

The summary represents the content of the South African science curriculum based on the National Curriculum and Assessment Policy Statement (CAPS). CAPS provides guidelines for teaching and learning in South African schools.

	Content domains	Process application
	Foundation phase	
Grade R	Beginning knowledge and social well-being	• Understanding good hygiene and healthy living • Recognising shapes and colours around us
	Creative arts	• Playing creative games • Improvising and interpreting visual art
	Physical education	• Walking, running and jumping • Throwing and catching beanbags
Grade 1	Social well-being	• Learning safety in the home • Developing an understanding of parts of body and senses • Learning and illustrating manners and responsibilities
	Creative arts	• Creating 2D and 3D art • Playing creative games • Making clay containers
	Physical education	• Rhyme singing while performing body actions • Engaging in jungle gym activities
Grade 2	Social well-being	• Recognising types of animals and creatures that live in water • Identifying different types of transport • Understanding road safety
	Creative arts	• Decorating clay containers • Playing creative games • Creating and playing with puppets
	Physical education	• Balancing exercise • Playing hopscotch • Playing tug-of-war
Grade 3	Social well-being	• Recycling • Understanding public safety • Learning the aspects of pollution
	Creative arts	• Listening and dancing to South African music • Clay modelling and decorating clay pots
	Physical education	• Sprinting • Long jump • Playing mini-cricket • Other sports

APPENDIX D:
Summary of South Africa's science curriculum

	Content domains	Process application
		Intermediate phase
Grade 4	Life and living	• Grasping the concept of living and non-living things • Understanding the structures of plants and animals • Identifying the habitats of animals
	Matter and materials	• Identifying and understanding materials around us • Differentiating solid materials
	Energy and change	• Understanding movement energy in a system • Developing knowledge on energy and sound transfer
	Planet Earth and beyond	• Understanding the overview of Planet Earth, sun and moon
Grade 5	Life and living	• Learning the different types of plants and animals on Earth • Recognising animal skeletons • Understanding the concept of life cycles
	Matter and materials	• Differentiating between metals and non-metals • Understanding the uses and processes of metals
	Energy and change	• Learning stored energy in fuels • Understanding energy and electricity
	Planet Earth and beyond	• Identifying Planet Earth
Grade 6	Life and living	• Understanding the concept of photosynthesis • Learning the different nutrients in food • Learning ecosystems and food webs
	Matter and materials	• Understanding the difference between solids, liquids and gases • Learning solutions as special mixtures
	Energy and change	• Recognising electric circuits • Understanding electrical conductors and insulators
	Planet Earth and beyond	• Understanding the solar system • Learning the systems for looking into space and exploring the moon and Mars
		Senior phase
Grade 7	Life and living	• Understanding the concept of the biosphere • Learning the types of animals and plants • Understanding human reproduction
	Matter and materials	• Recognising physical properties of materials • Applying methods of physical separation • Sorting and recycling materials • Understanding elements on the periodic table
	Energy and change	• Differentiating renewable and non-renewable sources of energy • Understanding potential and kinetic energy in systems • Learning the law of conservation of energy • Learning solar energy and life on Earth
	Planet Earth and beyond	• Understanding relative positions • Learning about gravity • Historical development of astronomy

	Content domains	Process application
Grade 8	Life and living	• Learning the concept of photosynthesis • Understanding respiration • Developing knowledge on ecosystems
	Matter and materials	• Types of micro-organisms • Mixtures of elements and compounds • Expansion and contraction of materials
	Energy and change	• Learning friction and static electricity • Understanding circuits and current electricity • Spectrum of visible light
	Planet Earth and beyond	• Recognising the sun and objects around the sun • Understanding Earth's position in the solar system • Learning about the Milky Way galaxy
Grade 8	Life and living	• Differentiating between plant and animal cells • Identifying systems in the human body • Understanding gaseous exchange
	Matter and materials	• Learning the periodic table • Learning names of compounds • Understanding chemical equations to represent reactions • Balancing equations
	Energy and change	• Recognising the different types of forces • Learning about electric cells • Understanding how electricity is generated • Understanding nuclear power in South Africa
	Planet Earth and beyond	• Learning the spheres of Earth • Understanding the process of mining in South Africa • Learning about the greenhouse effect

References

Adler J (1998) A Language of Teaching Dilemmas: Unlocking the Complex Multilingual Secondary Mathematics Classroom. *For the Learning of Mathematics 18*(1): 24-33

Adler J (1999) The dilemma of transparency: Seeing and seeing through talk in the mathematics classroom. *Journal for Research in Mathematics Education* 30(1): 47-64

Adler J (2006) *Teaching mathematics in multilingual classrooms* (Vol. 26): Springer: Science & Business Media

Banerjee A, Galiani S, Levinsohn J, McLaren Z & Woolard I (2009) Why has unemployment risen in the new South Africa? *Economics of Transition 16*(4): 715-740

Basic Education Laws Amendment Act (Act 15). (2011). *Basic Education Laws Amendment Act (Act 15 of 2011).* South Africa. Available at https://www.gov.za/sites/www.gov.za/files/a15_2011.pdf. [Accessed on 7 November 2017]

Bond TG & Fox CM (2015) *Applying the Rasch model: Fundamental measurement in the human sciences (3rd edition).* London: Lawrence Erlbaum Associates

Branson N & Hofmeyer C (2013) *Progress through school and the determinants of school dropout in South Africa.* Cape Town: SALDRU

Branson N, Lam D & Zuze TL (2012) *Education: Analysis of the NIDS Wave 1 and 2 Datasets.* Cape Town: SALDRU

Burton P & Leoschut L (2013) *School Violence in South Africa: Results of the 2012 National School Violence Study.* Cape Town: Centre for Justice and Crime Prevention

Caro DH, McDonald JT & Willms JD (2009) Socio-economic Status and Academic Achievement Trajectories from Childhood to Adolescence. *Canadian Journal of Education 32*(3): 558-590

Case A & Deaton A (1999) School Inputs and Educational Outcomes in South Africa. *The Quarterly Journal of Economics 114*(3): 1047-1084

Cates GL & Rhymer KN (2003) Examining the relationship between mathematics anxiety and mathematics performance: An instructional hierarchy perspective. *Journal of Behavioral Education 12*(1): 23-34

Cape Higher Education Consortium (2013) Pathways from university to work: *A graduate destination survey of the 2010 cohort of graduates from the Western Cape Universities.* Wynberg: CHEC

Central Applications Office (2017) Handbook 2018 Entry. Durban: Central Applications Office

Chisholm L (2013) The textbook saga and corruption in education. *Southern African Review of Education with Education with Production 19*(1): 7-22

Coleman JS, Campbell EQ, Hobson CJ, McPortland J, Mood AM, Weinfeld FD & York RL (1966), Equality of Educational Opportunity, Washington D.C., US. Dept. of Health, Education and Welfare, Office of Education/National Center for Education Statistics

Commission for Gender Equality (2007) *Gender in the curriculum.* Johannesburg: Commissiin for Gender Equality

Department of Basic Education (2010) *The National Policy for an Equitable Provision of an Enabling School Physical Teaching and Learning Environment.* Pretoria: Department of Basic Education

Department of Basic Education (2011a) *Action Plan to 2014: Towards the Realisation of Schooling 2025.* Pretoria: Department of Basic Education

Department of Basic Education (2011b) *National Education Infrastructure Management System Report.* Pretoria: Department of Basic Education

Department of Basic Education (2012a) *Guidelines Relating to Planning for Public School Infrastructure*. Pretoria: Department of Basic Education

Department of Basic Education (2012b) *National Guidelines for School Library and Information Services*. Pretoria: Department of Basic Education

Department of Basic Education (2013a) *Guide to Drug Testing in South African Schools*. Pretoria: Department of Basic Education

Department of Basic Education (2013b) *The Incremental Introduction of African Languages in South African Schools*. Draft Policy. Pretoria: Department of Basic Education

Department of Basic Education (2014) *Draft National Policy for the Provision and Management of Learning and Teaching Support Material (LTSM)*. Pretoria: Department of Basic Education

Department of Basic Education (2015a) Action Plan to 2019: *Towards the realisation of schooling 2030. Taking forward South Africa's National Development Plan 2030. Pretoria:* Department of Basic Education

Department of Basic Education (2015b) *National School Nutrition Programme 2013/14 Annual Report*. Pretoria: Department of Basic Education

Department of Basic Education (2015c) *The National School Safety Framework*. Pretoria: Department of Basic Education

Department of Basic Education (2015d) *School Safety/Violence & Bullying in Schools; Quality Learning and Teaching Campaign (QLTC) Implementation: progress report*. Pretoria: Department of Basic Education

Department of Basic Education (2016a) *Education Statistics in South Africa 2014*. Pretoria: Department of Basic Education

Department of Basic Education (2016b) *National Senior Certificate Examination Report 2016*. Pretoria: Department of Basic Education

Department of Basic Education (2016c) R*eport on progress in the schooling sector against key learner performance and attainment indicators*. Pretoria: Department of Basic Education

Department of Basic Education (2016d) *Revised Five Year Strategic Plan – 2015/16-2019/20*. Pretoria: Department of Basic Education

Department of Basic Education (2017a) *Safety in schools*. Pretoria: Department of Basic Education

Department of Basic Education (2017b) *School Infrastructure and Security Guidelines*. Pretoria: Department of Basic Education

Department of Education (1995) *White Paper on Education and Training*. Pretoria: Department of Education

Department of Education (2001a) *National Strategy for Mathematics, Science and Technology Education*. Pretoria: Department of Education

Department of Education (2001b) *National Strategy for Mathematics, Science and Technology Education in Gender and Further Education and Training*. Pretoria: Department of Education

Department of Education (2004) *White Paper on e-Education. Transforming Learning and Teaching through Information and Communication Technologies (ICTs)*. Pretoria: Department of Education

References

Department of Planning, Monitoring and Evaluation (2014) *Medium Term Strategic Framework: 2014-2019.* Pretoria: Department of Planning, Monitoring and Evaluation

Education Laws Amendment Act No. 50 (2002) *Education Laws Amendment Act (Act 50 of 2002)*

Eyal K & Woolard I (2013) *School Enrolment and the Child Support Grant: Evidence from South Africa.* Cape Town: NIDS

Fleisch B (2008) Primary education in crisis: Why South African schoolchildren underachieve in reading and mathematics. Cape Town: Juta and Company Ltd

Foley AE, Herts JB, Borgonovi F, Guerriero S, Levine SC & Beilock SL (2017) The Math Anxiety-Performance Link: A Global Phenomenon. *Current Directions in Psychological Science 26*(1): 52-58

Gauteng Department of Education (2012) *Exemplar School Safety Policy.* Johannesburg: Gauteng Department of Education

Gustafsson M (2016) *Understanding trends in high-level achievement in Grade 12 mathematics and physical science.* Stellenbosch: Research on Socio-Economic Policy

Gustafsson M & Patel F (2006) Undoing the apartheid legacy: Pro-poor spending shifts in the South African public school system. *Perspectives in education 24*(2): 65-77

Hanushek EA & Woessmann L (2015) *The Knowledge Capital of Nations: Education and the Economics of Growth.* Cambridge Massachusetts: MIT Press

Harris AL & Robinson K (2016) A New Framework for Understanding Parental Involvement: Setting the Stage for Academic Success. *Russell Sage Foundation Journal of the Social Sciences. 2*(5): 186-201. doi:10.7758/rsf.2016.2.5.09

Hoover-Dempsey KV, Battiato AC, Walker JMT, Reed RP, DeJong JM & Jones KP (2001) Parental Involvement in Homework. *Educational Psychologist 36*(3): 195-209. doi:10.1207/S15326985EP3603_5

Hox J (2010) Multilevel Analysis. *Techniques and Applications.* New York: Routledge

Lee VE, Zuze TL & Ross K (2005) *School effectiveness in 14 sub-Saharan African countries: Links with 6 th Graders' reading achievement.* (Vol. 31)

Lee VE & Zuze TL (2011) School Resources and Academic Performance in Sub-Saharan Africa. *Comparative Education Review 55*(3): 369-397

Lubienski ST, Robinson JP, Crane CC & Ganley CM (2013) Girls' and Boys' Mathematics Achievement, Affect, and Experiences: Findings from ECLS-K. *National Council of Teachers of Mathematics 44*(4): 634-645

McCamey R (2002) *A primer for the one-parameter Rasch model.* Paper presented at the Annual Meeting of the Southwest Educational Research Association, Austin, Texas

Mouton J, Boshoff N, James M & Treptow R (2010) ASSAF *Tracer Study of University Graduates in the Social Sciences, Humanities and Arts.* Stellenbosch: National Institute for the Human and Social Sciences

Mullis IVS, Martin MO, Foy P & Hooper M (2016) *TIMSS 2015 International Results in Mathematics.* Boston: TIMSS & PIRLS International Study Center

National Planning Commission (2011) *National Development Plan: Vision for 2030.* Pretoria: The Presidency

OECD (2013a) *PISA 2012 Results: Excellence Through Equity: Giving Every Student the Chance to Succeed (Volume II)*. Paris: OECD

OECD (2013b) *Ready to Learn: Students' Engagement, Drive and Self-Beliefs - Volume II*. Paris: OECD

PISA (2016) *Equations and Inequalities. Making Mathematics Accessible to All*. Paris: OECD

Probyn M (2009) 'Smuggling the vernacular into the classroom': conflicts and tensions in classroom codeswitching in township/rural schools in South Africa. *International Journal of Bilingual Education and Bilingualism 12*(2): 123-136. doi:10.1080/13670050802153137

Raudenbush SW & Bryk AS (2002) *Hierarchical linear models: Applications and data analysis methods*. London: Sage

Reddy V, Visser M., Winnaar L., Arends F., Juan A., Prinsloo CH & Isdale K (2016a) *TIMSS 2015. Highlights of Mathematics and Science Achievement of Grade 9 South African Learners. Nurturing Green Shoots*. Pretoria: Human Sciences Research Council

Reddy V, Bhorat H, Powell M, Visser M & Arends F (2016b) *Skills Supply and Demand in South Africa*. Pretoria: HSRC

Reddy V, Juan A, Zuze TL, Namome C & Hannan S (2016c) Does it matter if students enjoy learning science? Exploring student attitudes towards science in South Africa. *TIMSS SA Policy Briefs*. Pretoria: HSRC

Reddy V, Kanjee A, Diedericks G & Winnaar L (2006) *Mathematics and science achievement at South African schools in TIMSS 2003*. Pretoria: HSRC

Reddy V, Prinsloo CH, Netshitangani T, Moletsane R, Juan A & Janse van Rensburg D (2010) An investigation into educator leave in the South African ordinary public schooling system. Pretoria: HSRC

Reddy V, Zuze T, Visser M, Winnaar L, Juan A, Prinsloo C & Rogers S (2015) *Beyond benchmarks: What twenty years of TIMSS data tell us about South African education:* HSRC Press

Rodwell P (2015) 8 Aspects of a positive school climate & culture. Available at https://www.kickboardforschools.com/blog/post/8-aspects-of-a-positive-school-climate-culture. [Accessed on 6 November 2017]

Roksa J & Potter D (2011) Parenting and Academic Achievement: Intergenerational Transmission of Educational Advantage. *Sociology of Education 84*(4): 299-321

Rumberger RW & Palardy GJ (2004). Multilevel models of School Effectiveness Research. In D. Kaplan (Ed.), Handbook of Quantitative Methodology for the Social Sciences (pp. 235-258). Thousand Oaks, CA: Sage Publishers

SACMEQ. (2010) *How successful are textbook provision programmes?* Paris: SACMEQ

SASSA (2017) *Statistical Report 4 of 2017 – 30 April 2017.* Pretoria: South African Social Security Agency SASSA

Scherman V, Long C, Coetzee C & Abrie M (2017) *Establishing Benchmarks. Using TIMSS performance data to create relevant benchmarks for South Africa*. Unpublished manuscript

Sebastian J, Moon JM & Cunningham M (2017) The relationship of school-based parental involvement with student achievement: a comparison of principal and parent survey reports from PISA 2012. *Educational Studies, 43*(2): 123-146

Setati M & Adler J (2000) Between languages and discourses: Language practices in primary multilingual mathematics classrooms in South Africa. *Educational Studies in Mathematics, 43*(3): 243-269

References

Snijders T & Bosker R (1999) Multilevel analysis: An introduction to basic and applied multilevel analysis. London: Sage

Stats SA (2016) *Community Survey 2016 in Brief.* Statistics South Africa. Pretoria: SSA

Swars SL, Daane C & Giesen J (2006) Mathematics anxiety and mathematics teacher efficacy: What is the relationship in elementary preservice teachers? *School Science and Mathematics, 106*(7): 306-315

Taylor S & Yu D (2009) The importance of socio-economic status in determining educational achievement in South Africa. *Unpublished Working Paper (Economics). Stellenbosch: Stellenbosch University.*

Thapa A, Cohen J, Higgins-D'Alessandro A & Guffey S (2012) *School climate research summary: August 2012.* New York: National School Climate Center

The Constitution of the Republic of South Africa (1996) Constitution of the Republic of South Africa. Pretoria: Government Printer

Thien LM & Ong MY (2015) Malaysian and Singaporean students' affective characteristics and mathematics performance: evidence from PISA 2012 *SpringerPlus 4:* 563

Traub RE & Wolfe RG (1981) Latent Trait Theories and the Assessment of Educational Achievement. *Review of Research in Education 9:* 377-435

United Nations (2017) *The Sustainable Development Goals Report.* Retrieved from New York: UN

Van der Berg S (2008) How effective are poor schools? Poverty and educational outcomes in South Africa. *Studies in Educational Evaluation 34*(3): 145-154

Veriava F (2013) *The 2012 Limpopo Book Crisis.* Johannesburg: Section 27

Visser M, Juan A & Feza N (2015) Home and school resources as predictors of mathematics performance in South Africa. *South African Journal of Education 35*(1): 1-10

Wang M & Sheikh-Khalil S (2014) Does Parental Involvement Matter for Student Achievement and Mental Health in High School? *Child development 85*(2): 610-625

Watt L (2016) Engaging hard to reach families: learning from five 'outstanding' schools. *Education 3-13 44*(1): 32-43

Wilder S (2014) Effects of parental involvement on academic achievement: a meta-synthesis. *Educational Review 66*(3): 377-397

Zieky MJ (2012) So much has changed. In Cizek GJ (Ed.), *Setting performance standards: Foundations, methods and innovations.* London: Routledge

Zuze TL & Leibbrandt M (2011) Free education and social inequality in Ugandan primary schools: A step backward or a step in the right direction? *International Journal of Educational Development 31*(2): 169-178

Zuze TL & Reddy V (2014) School resources and the gender reading literacy gap in South African schools. *International Journal of Educational Development 36* (Supplement C): 100-107

Zuze TL, Reddy V, Juan A, Hannan S, Visser M & Winnaar L (2016) Safe and sound?: violence and South African education. *TIMSS SA Policy Briefs*

Zuze TL, Reddy V, Juan A, Visser M, Winnaar L & Hannan S (2015) *Have we reached gender equity in mathematics education? Evidence from TIMSS South Africa 2011*

Index

Index